The Art of
Wire
Creative Techniques for Designer Jewelry

J. Marsha Michler

KRAUSE PUBLICATIONS
Cincinnati, Ohio

contents

introduction

Wire is rich in possibility and gives you endless opportunities to create artful jewelry. Wire can be shaped in infinite ways, opening up a world of design options ranging from flat forms to sculptural ones. Different techniques yield different results. If filigree techniques are used, finished pieces clearly show their wire roots, but aligning wire in wire wrapping gives wire the look of solid metal, while dowel knitting and crochet make wire look almost like cloth. Try your hand at some or all of the techniques presented in this book. Wrap, hammer, coil, curl, twist, dowel knit and crochet your way through the pages of this book to make your own fabulous jewelry.

Wire working is an art and a craft that anyone with a few simple tools can pursue. Only a simple workshop setup is needed; attractive, wearable pieces are entirely attainable with minimal space and expense. As you dive into making jewelry from wire, begin with Chapter One for background on the materials, tools and techniques essential to successful wire working. If you're an absolute beginner, learn to make plain and wrapped loops first (see pages 19–20), then broaden your horizons with additional techniques.

Once you're ready to start creating, venture into the project chapters. Each chapter features a different way to work with wire. The chapters are in no formal order, although each begins with an easy piece especially designed to teach a skill. Start with the first project in each chapter to learn the featured technique, then try other projects in the chapter that appeal to you. Explore all of the techniques! Chances are that you will find one or more that appeal to you. You can even combine techniques to make original designs.

Creating stunning jewelry using wire is an ageless art and craft. Some of the pieces in this book were inspired by ancient jewelry on display at the Louvre Museum. These early wire-formed pieces were meticulously crafted and impressed me as something to aspire to in my own work. The designs seemed timeless—as wearable today as they were in their own day. I've tried to present designs here that have a similar timeless quality. I hope that in these pages you find inspiring ideas and fun things to try and that you'll use the techniques in this book to develop ideas for your own original jewelry designs.

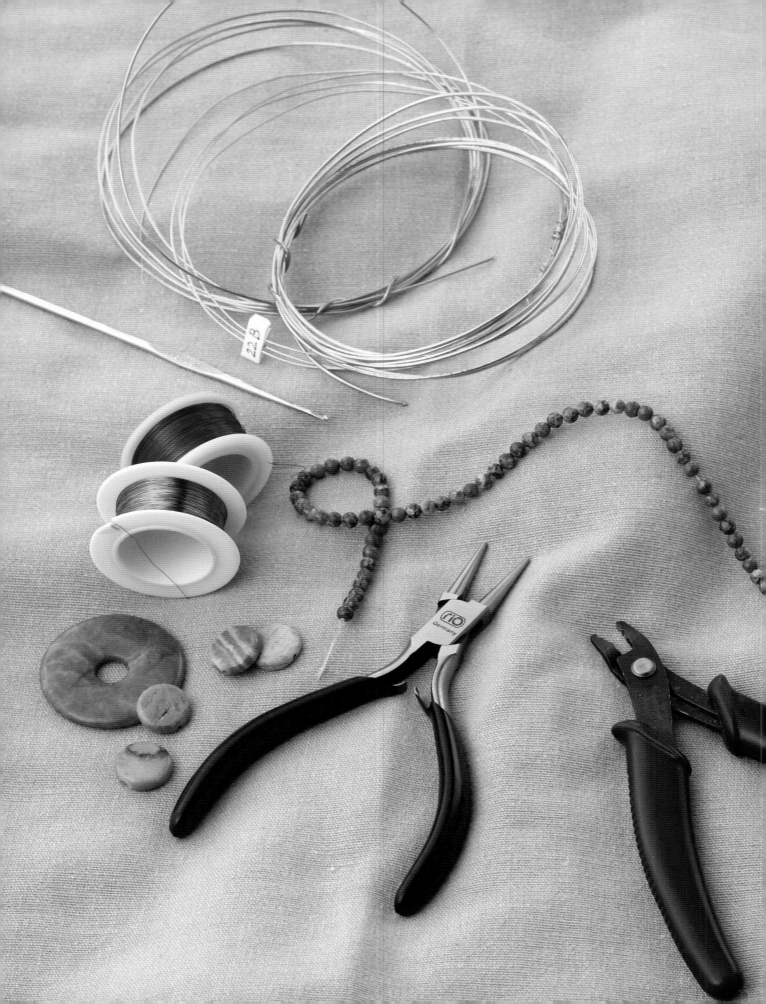

getting started

In this chapter you will learn all that you need to know before you begin creating the projects in the following chapters. In these pages you'll find information regarding jewelry making materials, tools and workspaces, as well as wire working techniques. Before the technique lessons we'll also discuss safety, which is enormously important. Please take a moment to read this section on page 15.

Before you start making jewelry, you'll need to have tools and supplies. There are almost endless choices in both of these areas, and picking materials and tools can be daunting if you're not armed with information. We'll first discuss the many aspects of wire, which is used in every project throughout this book. We'll also cover materials like beads and findings. After that we'll discuss tools, including which ones you must have on hand and which ones you might find useful, but not necessary. Finally, before we dive into techniques, we'll look at setting up a workspace for yourself. Setting up a workspace makes creating an easy thing to do. The more serious you get about making wire jewelry, the more important your materials, tools and workspace become.

Once you're ready to begin working I'll show you wire working techniques. Some, like cutting wire and finishing wire ends, will be important to all projects. Spend time practicing these frequently used techniques and you will be on your way to becoming a master of your craft. This section also includes step-by-step instructions for basic wire shaping and shows you how to create your own findings. Although findings may be purchased, you also have the option of creating your own. Have fun and experiment with designing your own findings—make them a part of a finished piece, not just an add-on.

Once you've been through this chapter, you'll be ready to make your own wire jewelry.

materials

The items you use to create your jewelry pieces can be as simple or as splendid as you desire. Supplies are available in a wide range of materials, colors, sizes and price ranges. The information over the following pages will help you to pick the right pieces for your projects.

Wire

Wire is used in all of the projects in this book to create both the structure of the jewelry pieces and the decorative elements. Base metal wires are sold by length or weight, and gold and silver are priced based on the market price for the metal used to make the wire, plus a markup added by a seller. There are many different factors to consider when choosing wire for your project, including metal, gauge, shape and hardness.

Metal

The metals used to create wire can be divided into two categories: base metals and precious metals. Base metals include brass, copper and nickel silver. I recommend using base metals when you are practicing a technique and when you are working a new design for the first time. These inexpensive wires can be scrapped if a project doesn't work out. Any of the base metal wires can be used to make finished jewelry. Precious metals include silver and gold. Because of their higher value, use gold or silver wire for fine, finished pieces. Both gold and silver wire are sold by weight, and the price can change daily, depending on the market.

Brass

Brass is an alloy consisting of copper and zinc. Different types of brass are made by varying the proportions of copper to zinc; an alloy with 15 percent zinc is often used for jewelry making. This alloy goes by several names including rich low brass and Merlin's gold. Jeweler's bronze is another name often used; this alloy has a color similar to 14k gold. Brass tarnishes, but more slowly than pure copper. Yellow brass, consisting of 30 percent zinc, may also be used for jewelry. This alloy is more yellow in color than rich low brass.

Copper

Most copper wire used for jewelry making is pure, or 99.9 percent pure. A softer metal than brass, it is very malleable and easy to shape, file and saw. When filed or sanded, copper appears pinkish but soon tarnishes to a deeper reddish or brownish hue. Outdoors, exposed to the elements, copper naturally weathers through shades of russet brown and gradually to green and finally to a light green you may sometimes see on antique roofs or weather vanes. Bronze and brass, because they contain copper, will also form this patina. These color changes cannot be expected to naturally occur on jewelry, however. Patinating copper jewelry requires application of chemicals, and sometimes the heat of a torch.

Copper wires can be coated with different materials that give the wire a color. Use these for projects that will not be hammered or filed as the coating will be removed by these processes.

Nickel Silver

Nickel silver, also called German silver, is an alloy of 60 percent copper, 20 percent nickel and 20 percent zinc. There is not actually any silver in it. Much less malleable than brass or copper, nickel silver is good for a design that you want to look silver when you don't want to actually use silver wire. Although it is widely used in commercially produced costume jewelry, nickel silver triggers allergic reactions in some people, most notably when used in ear wires.

Fine Silver, Sterling Silver and Argentium Sterling

Fine silver is pure and it is very malleable—only slightly harder than gold. Although significantly less expensive than gold, it is still a precious metal. Sterling silver is an alloy containing 92.5 percent silver and 7.5 percent of another metal, such as copper. The added metal has a strengthening effect, since pure silver (or 99.9 percent pure) is relatively soft. Sterling silver tarnishes as a result of the metals in the alloy other than the silver reacting to oxygen in the air. If you prefer to work with silver that won't tarnish easily, use Argentium. This is a relatively new alloy of silver and germanium.

Gold and Gold Fill

Gold is the most malleable of the metals. Pure gold is bright metallic yellow. It is often alloyed with another metal to harden it and change the color. Adding copper makes a reddish alloy, silver makes a greenish alloy, and palladium or nickel make a white alloy. Copper is the most commonly used additive. Alloys lower the caratage, or amount of pure gold, and are rated by the amount of pure gold in the alloy. A higher caratage number denotes a higher percentage of pure gold (for instance, 24k gold contains more gold than 14k gold).

Gold-filled, or rolled gold, wire consists of an outer layer of gold bonded to a core of non-precious metal such as brass or nickel. The durability of the gold surface varies, but will usually hold up for twenty to thirty years with daily wear.

Gauge

The word gauge refers to the thickness of a wire, and is measured according to the American Wire Gauge (AWG) system. This system is also known as the Brown & Sharpe, or B&S. Most base metal wires come in a range of round gauges. Wire is sometimes also specified in millimeters or thousandths of an inch, but we will be using the AWG system in this book.

When measuring gauge, the lower the number, the heavier the wire. Gauges 16, 18, 20, 22 and 24 are used in many of the projects in this book. Finer gauges such as 26, 28, 30, 32 and 34 are used for dowel knitting and crochet.

Shape

While most wire is round, some wires are also available in different shapes. Twisted, square and half-round shapes are widely available, and some vendors even offer wide patterned strips of wire.

The angles inherent in square wire create variety in designs, but keep in mind that the squared edges tend to be a bit sharp and may not be comfortable to wear next to the skin. Half-round wire is often used for wire wrapping, although round wire may be used instead. Twisted wire is easy to make yourself, so I suggest making your own rather than buying it. Making your own twisted wire gives you the added bonus of customization—you can combine different colors, shapes and gauges of wire if you desire.

Hardness

Wire comes in three different hardnesses: dead soft, half-hard and hard. Dead soft wire is preferred for most wire working, and base metal wires are most often available this way. Wire naturally hardens as it is worked. You can feel wire stiffen as you bend, twist and hammer it. Most pieces will be sturdy enough to wear just from the shaping and bending that is done during assembly.

Bits of Gold, Bits of Silver

Cut-off bits and filings of precious metals such as silver and gold are typically melted down and reused. If you don't have the equipment for doing this, there are companies that buy precious metal scrap; some jewelry suppliers will do this. Keep your silver and gold scraps sorted in containers dedicated to the individual metals.

I also keep a coffee can on my workbench to catch base metal scraps. Your local recycling facility will know what to do with a can of scrap.

Beads, Cabochons and Donuts

Beads come in many materials, colors and shapes and a range of sizes; each bead has a hole in it for stringing. Hole sizes in beads vary, even within a single strand of beads. When you are buying beads to use on wire, first check that your wire will fit through the hole in the beads. Save the ones that don't fit for projects using finer wire or beading threads.

Cabochons are smooth, domed stones with flat backs; they are usually placed into a setting. Cabochons are available in a range of sizes and are most often round or oval shaped.

Donut beads are disks that feature a large hole in the center. They make a perfect focal point for a necklace, especially when attached with an attractive bail.

Beads, cabochons and donuts can be made of crystal, glass, stone, shell, bone, wood, cloisonné and other materials. This includes a wide range of semiprecious stones including jade, amethyst, agate, moonstone, quartz, malachite, onyx, citrine, garnet, fluorite and many others. The natural beauty of these stones can be set off nicely by a compatible wire color.

For the projects in this book, collect an assortment of beads in addition to the cabochons and donuts called for in the projects. All are widely available through jewelry supply shops and websites. I recommend that when you see beads that you like, purchase them. Then you will have a variety to choose from when you feel the urge to create a new piece of jewelry.

Findings

Findings are used to assemble jewelry, and include crimp beads, jump rings, pin backs, ear wires and clasps. Except for crimp beads, you can make all of these findings yourself. Instructions for these items can be found on pages 23–29. I think that handmade findings are the finish of integrity for handwrought jewelry. If you prefer to purchase findings, they are widely available through craft stores and beading supply stores.

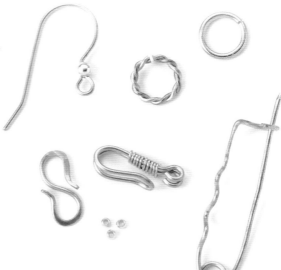

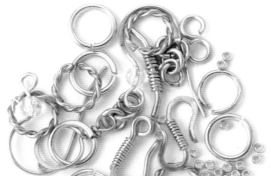

tools

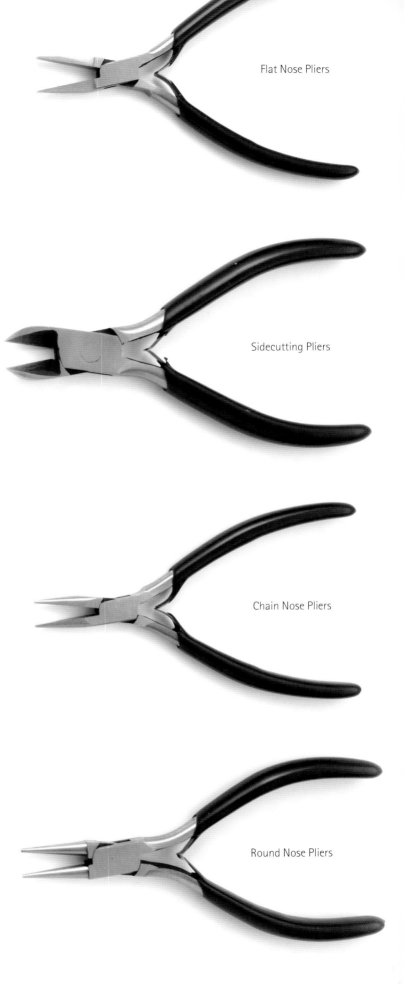

Flat Nose Pliers

Sidecutting Pliers

Chain Nose Pliers

Round Nose Pliers

Pliers

A set of chain nose, flat nose and round nose pliers, plus a pair of wire cutters, are essential to wire working. Chain nose pliers have tapered jaws with flat surfaces. They are used for many wire bending and shaping tasks, and for opening and closing loops and jump rings.

Flat nose pliers have square jaws with flat surfaces. They are used for bending wire to form angles, flattening wire, and for use in conjunction with chain nose pliers when you need to work with a pair of pliers in each hand.

Round nose pliers have tapered, round jaws. They are used for forming rounded bends and loops. The tapered jaw makes it possible to form loops of varying sizes.

Sidecutting pliers are a cutting tool with short, sharp jaws. The cut leaves one edge of the wire nearly flat and the other with a slight V shape. Cutters are rated for their maximum cutting capacity, which is the heaviest gauge of wire that can be cut with the pliers. For the projects in this book you will need cutters rated for 16 gauge wire.

Unlike multipurpose pliers and cutters made for household and building uses, jewelry tools are light-weight, compact, and have smooth jaws to prevent wire marring. Choose a set that fits your hand comfortably. Some pliers are made with padded handles, or are shaped ergonomically to better fit your hand. You will need a good fit if you plan on any prolonged use of a tool.

It is possible for beginners to get by with inexpensive tools, but I suggest you step up to higher quality as your skills improve. Quality makes a big difference in accuracy and ease of use. I recommend shopping where there is a selection of quality brands—this allows you to try a variety and choose the pair that works best for you.

Throughout this book, it is assumed that you will have these four types of pliers on your bench in front of you and handy at all times, along with a metal ruler. (These items are not listed in the items needed to complete a project.)

Additional Tools

The tools listed below and pictured on the next page should also be a part of your tool collection, although some have more specific uses than others. Most are available from a jewelry supplier, and some can be found at a hardware store.

Crimping pliers **(1)** are used to shape a crimp bead so that it firmly holds beading wire **(2)**. Crimping pliers work by first flattening, then folding a crimping bead. A pair of chain nose or flat nose pliers may be used instead to simply flatten the crimp bead, but the results will not be as tidy.

A planishing hammer **(3)** has a smooth, flat head that is perfect for flattening wire. Opposite the flat surface is a rounded one that can be used to create rounded forms and to dimple metal to create texture. I do my hammering with a small carpenter's hammer **(4)** instead, and I find that it works just as well. A rawhide mallet **(5)** is useful for work hardening wire without changing its surface.

An anvil **(6)** is used to support your jewelry pieces while you are working them with a hammer or mallet. You can purchase an avil that clamps onto the edge of a workbench or table, or you can use a simple block of metal and place it on your work surface. A jeweler's vise **(7)** is used for twisting wire and for sawing jump rings. A vise specially made for jewelry is small and has smooth jaws to prevent marring metal. There are types that clamp onto the side of the workbench, those that are fastened on using screws, and some even have a vacuum base. Some swivel, and very fancy ones also tilt, but all you need for wire working is a basic one.

A flat needle file **(8)** or an emery cloth **(9)** can be used for removing burs and smoothing cut ends of wire. Use a file in one direction only—by pushing it forward. A sawing action will dull the file. A bastard file **(10)**, also called a mill bastard, is a serious metal-mover. Use it to sharpen wire into a pin end and to flatten the ends of jump rings that are made using side cutters. A bastard file can be found at a hardware store.

A jeweler's saw **(11)** is used for making your own jump rings (see Jump Rings on pages 23–24). Buy the highest quality blades you can afford—cheap ones tend to break easily. To place the blade in the frame, orient it with the teeth pointed toward the handle, then fasten the blade into the upper end of the frame (away from the handle). Next, push on the frame while fastening the lower end. This ensures that the blade will be taut. Use a size 0 or size 1 blade for 20 gauge wire and a size 2 blade for 18 gauge and 16 gauge wire.

A drawplate **(12)** is a finishing tool for dowel knitting. It is used for smoothing and lengthening the knitted tube. These tools feature a series of holes that range from a $\frac{1}{2}$" (1.3cm) diameter to approximately $\frac{1}{8}$" (3mm) in diameter. You can make your own using a drill, a set of bits and a piece of hardwood. To use a drawplate, fasten it in a bench vise or hold it firmly while you pull the knitted tube through the smallest hole it will fit through.

Dowels **(13)**, a ring mandrel **(14)** and other round objects such as nails **(15)** are needed for dowel knitting and various shaping tasks as well as for making jump rings and coils. I suggest purchasing several dowel rods from a hardware store—get one each of every size with a $\frac{1}{2}$" (1.3cm) diameter and smaller. Cut a 6" (15.2cm) length from each (it's fine to use your jeweler's saw for this). Nails or the handle of a needle file are useful for making jump rings. A crochet hook **(16)** is used to crochet wire in Chapter Five.

A wire twisting tool **(17)** is used to twist a single square wire or to twist together two or more lengths of wire. To learn how to use the tool see page 31. A wire jig **(18)** is a pegboard with movable pegs **(19)** that can be used to shape wire. While the projects in this book do not require a jig, it is a handy gadget if you want to repeatedly make the same shape.

A rouge cloth **(20)** is used for polishing wire. The cloth is permeated with a metal polishing agent. Use the cloth to clean wire before using it, and for polishing finished pieces. Do not use a rouge cloth on coated wire, beads or stones—it is abrasive and can mar finishes. The rouge cloth comes backed with a plain cloth, which can be used on coated wire.

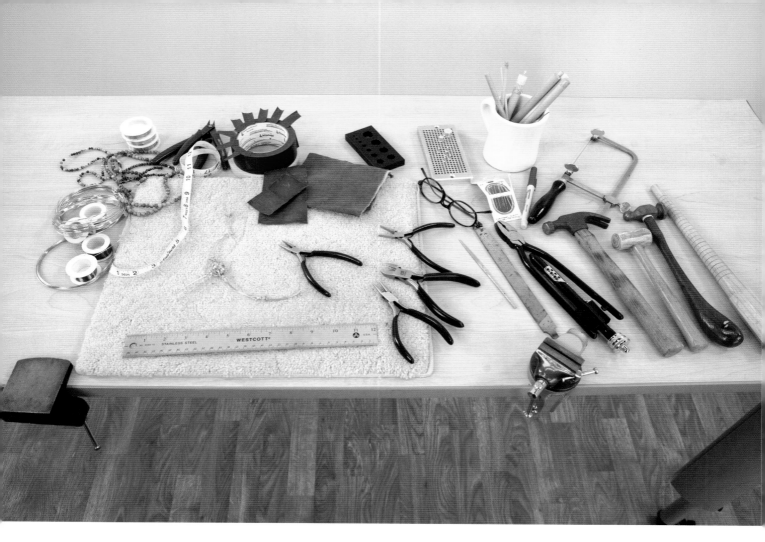

workspace

I strongly recommend keeping a dedicated space for jewelry making. An optimal workspace should have a table or a desk to serve as a workbench and wall space for a pegboard or shelves. Good lighting and comfortable seating are essential, especially during a long jewelry-making session. You'll also need some drawers or space to stack boxes of beads and other supplies. A source of magnification can be very helpful as well; keep reading glasses or a magnifying lamp on hand. This makes it easier to do a good job of finishing off wire ends and other detailed tasks.

In my own workspace, I like to work over a carpet sample. It keeps beads and small parts from rolling away, and captures tiny snipped ends of wire. I keep small items like jump rings sorted in a divided dish, dowels and nails in a coffee mug, and commonly used tools close at hand. My spools of base metal wire are kept on large nails on the wall in front of me, where they're ready for me to grab and use. I store precious metal wires in protective wrappings in a drawer. Beads and cabochons are stacked in plastic divided boxes that snap shut securely. My anvil and jeweler's vise are clamped onto the workbench, handy to use as needed.

If you are a beginner you may find your space evolving to fit your needs—let it happen! Strive for a combination of comfort and utility; your workspace should fit you.

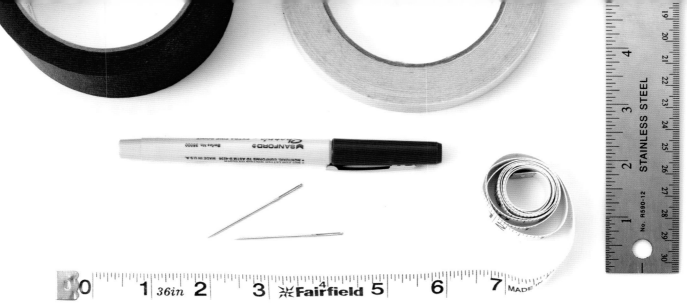

Other Supplies

In addition to the tools already mentioned, you should also have the following items on hand: a metal ruler with inches and millimeters, a tape measure, permanent marker, painter's tape, masking tape and tapestry sewing needles.

Before you begin a project that requires tape, cut off several tabs so that you have them ready for you when you need them.

Safety

Before we turn to discussing techniques, we need to discuss safety precautions. Safety is too important to ignore, especially when following a few simple steps will keep you crafting happily. First, always wear safety glasses when you are working with wire. Never let a bit of wire go flying as it is cut. Hold your free hand over the cut being made, or make sure that the wire on either side of the cutters is held in some way. Cut wire has sharp edges that cannot be seen easily. Finish wire ends by sanding or filing them smooth as soon as a cut is made.

Even with these precautions, occasional small cuts are inevitable. Keep your tetanus vaccine up to date, and a box of bandages handy. Keep food and drink out of your workspace. Clean up thoroughly after each work session, and vacuum up all small bits of wire. Store all tools, wires, beads and other supplies out of reach of small children.

In addition to taking care with tools and materials, also consider the design of each jewelry piece that you make. Wire is solid metal capable of forming into an unbreakable structure unless there is a breaking point or some easy exit for the piece. Bracelets and necklaces should always be made with areas that will come apart if the jewelry should become caught on something as it is being worn. Use unsoldered jump rings to fasten on clasps, and make a type of ear wire that slides out of the ear readily.

basic techniques & findings

If you are new to wire work, begin by practicing the techniques in this section before going on to the projects. These are basic skills that are used in many of the projects.

Developing skill in wire working requires repetition more than anything else. Focus on shaping the wire and molding the pieces to resemble the ones you see in the photos. For now, don't concern yourself with the nicks and scratches in the wire that are sure to occur. Once you achieve some proficiency in working with wire, the surface marks will be less of an issue. Jewelry making is a craft, and the only way to master a craft is with lots of practice. So, don't start by expecting or looking for perfection—just learn the moves for now and your work will improve as you gain skill.

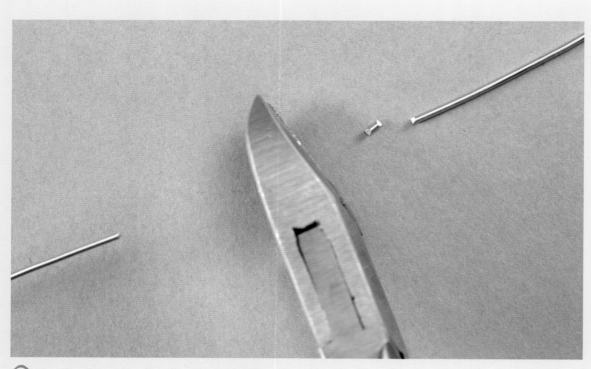

Beginning a Wire Project

A couple of quick steps before you start working will get your project on the right path.

First, before cutting a length of wire, uncoil the amount needed, grasp the wire near the spool or coil with a rouge cloth and pull the wire through the cloth. (For coated wires use a plain cloth.) Repeat this step until the wire is straight. This both straightens and cleans the wire and is usually only needed for heavier wire gauges. Finer gauges (26–34 gauge) can usually be used straight off the spool as they are.

Next, cut the length of wire needed. The cut edge that lies against the flat side of the cutters is the useable wire end, so cut with the flat side of the cutters toward the spool. Then, turn the pliers and recut the wire with the flat side of the cutters to remove the V-shaped end. This will ensure that both ends of your wire are flat-cut. If you choose, you can file down the V-shaped cut end instead, but it is quicker and easier to simply recut the end to make it flat.

Finally, check the wire ends for burs or sharp edges and use a needle file or emery cloth to smooth them away.

Wrapping

Wrapping is used in many jewelry pieces either as a decorative element or to fasten wires together. If you learn to wrap wire neatly, it will greatly contribute to the overall look of your jewelry. Some jewelry makers prefer using half-round wire for wrapping, but I generally find it easier to keep my supplies to a minimum and use round wire for wrapping. The wire gauges used most often for wrapping are 22 gauge and 24 gauge.

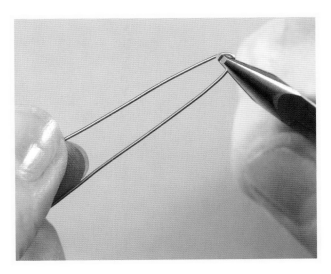

1 Use a pair of chain nose pliers to bend the wrapping wire in half.

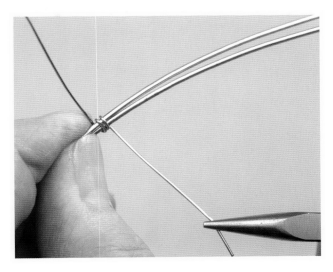

2 Place the bend over the length or lengths of wire to be wrapped. Bring one end of the wrapping wire around using chain nose pliers and wrap snugly. If you are wrapping around a single wire, leave an end on the wrapping wire and hold onto it as you wrap to keep the wire from swiveling (if the wire swivels it isn't wrapping).

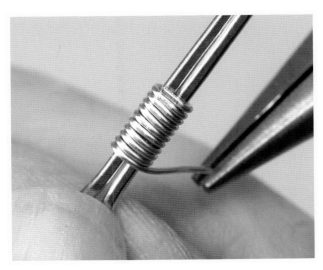

3 Wrap using the other end of the wrapping wire. Finish the ends of a wrap by using chain nose pliers to pinch the wire ends tightly against the wrapped wire. You can hammer the wraps lightly to secure them (see Hammering on page 18).

Other Wrapping Options

These instructions show a wrap that is started in the center and worked outward. Wrapping can also begin at one end of the wrap, rather than at the center. To work a wrap end to end, begin wrapping approximately 1" (2.5cm) from the end of the wire. Create the number of wraps needed, then trim off any excess wire.

Hammering

Hammering serves many purposes in jewelry making. First, it work hardens the wire; as it is worked, metal tightens up, making it hold its shape. Bending, twisting and hammering all work harden wire. Hammering can also be used to flatten wire, to settle pieces into place or to add texture to the wire.

Hammer the wire on an anvil in a series of light taps using the flexibility of your wrist, not the force of your arm. Use a rawhide mallet to set the wraps and wire components into place and lightly work harden the wire. A rawhide mallet is a light duty tool only; it is not made to flatten wire.

Use a planishing hammer or a small carpenter's hammer to flatten the wire. Keep the hammer head parallel to the anvil and pound lightly until the desired degree of flatness is achieved. When flattening, hammer on the wrong side to reduce hammer dents on the face of the finished piece.

Finishes for Wire Jewelry

Experiment with different ways to put a finish on wire pieces. I tend to like the hammered look, which leaves shimmery, flat surfaces that catch the light. Hammering gives a piece a forged look. Try hammering with the rounded end of a planishing hammer to create dents. Experiment with filing the surface with a diamond needle file or fine jeweler's sandpapers to create brushed surfaces. Buff your finished pieces using a rouge cloth (uncoated wires only).

Loops

Forming a loop is a very important technique to learn in wire working. Loops are so often used that it is easy to take them for granted, but a perfectly formed loop is a sign of quality. If you need practice at making loops, make lots of bead links (see Bead Links and Bead Drops on pages 21–22) and join them into bracelets and necklaces. Following are instructions for the different types of loops used in this book.

Plain Loops

A plain loop is very basic and easy to make. This type of loop can be opened at any time, so it can used easily to connect different jewelry elements. A plain loop requires approximately $^3/_8"$–$^1/_2"$ (1cm–1.3cm) of 18 to 20 gauge wire, depending on the size of the loop.

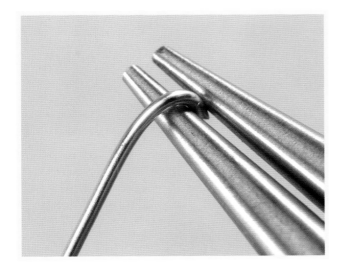

1 Begin by cutting the wire flat (see Beginning a Wire Project on page 16). Using a pair of round nose pliers, grasp the very end of the wire. Check that no wire protrudes beyond the jaws of the pliers. Turn your wrist away from yourself. Reposition the pliers and continue turning as needed until a complete loop forms.

2 Change to a pair of chain nose pliers. Grasp the loop at its base and turn your wrist until the loop is centered over the wire.

Loop Consistency

The jaws of round nose pliers are graduated, so the size of your loop will be determined by the part of the jaw you wrap your wire on. If you wrap toward the tip, you'll form a smaller loop, and if you wrap toward the handle you'll form a larger loop. If you are making several loops and want them to match, mark the place on the pliers where you are making your loops with a scratch or a piece of masking tape. Continue making the loops at the same place on the pliers and they'll all be the same size.

Wrapped Loops

A wrapped loop forms a secure, permanently closed connection. Wraps can be done one, two or more times. Using 20 gauge wire, a wrapped loop that is wrapped three times takes about 1" (2.5cm) of wire. Adjust the length of wire according to the gauge of the wire and the number of wraps needed.

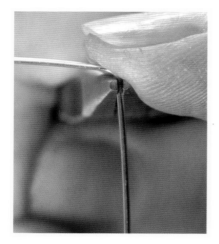

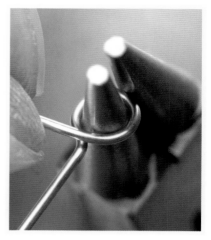

1 Measure 1" (2.5cm) in from the end of the wire and place your thumbnail there. Grasp the wire next to your thumbnail with a pair of chain nose pliers. Using your thumb, push the wire over the top of the pliers, bending it into a 90 degree angle.

2 Grasp at the bend with a pair of round nose pliers and bring the wire end over the top of the pliers.

3 Turn the pliers to grasp the top of the started loop. Bring the wire under the jaw of the pliers. A complete loop is formed.

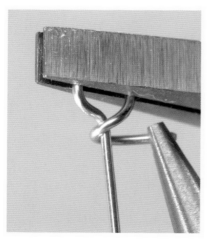

4 Clamp the loop with a pair of flat nose pliers; using a pair of chain nose pliers, bring the wire end around in a series of even wraps at the base of the loop.

5 Use the chain nose pliers to tuck the wire end tightly against the wraps.

Joining Wrapped Loops

If you are joining a wrapped loop to another jewelry piece, follow Steps 1–3 on this page, then fasten the open loop onto whatever you are joining it to. Finish the wrapped loop with Steps 4–5 on this page. Use round nose pliers in place of flat nose pliers for Step 4.

Tight Loops

You will see the words "fasten with a tight loop" often throughout this book. This is a neat, clean and secure way of fastening one wire onto another. Double check that you are placing a loop in the correct place before you begin since these can be difficult to reopen. Work tight loops in practice wire until you are proficient at them.

1 Use a pair of round nose pliers to start a loop in the end of the wire that will be fastened on.

2 Place the started loop onto the other wire; use a pair of chain nose pliers to close the loop. The loop should go all the way around the other wire and should be fitted snugly.

Bead Links and Bead Drops

Once you've mastered loops you can use them to create bead links and bead drops, essential components for wire jewelry. Links have a loop at each end and are used to fasten pieces together. A chain can be made of links by fastening one onto another to create the length needed. Use drops, which have a loop only at one end, for bracelet charms, as pendants, or attach them to ear wires to make earrings.

Bead Links

These links are made with plain loops. These can be attached to or taken off of jewelry at any time simply by opening the loop as if it were a jump ring (see Opening and Closing Jump Rings on page 24). To make a bead link with a plain loop at each end, form a plain loop in one end of the wire, string on the bead, then form a plain loop in the remaining end. If you are using 20 gauge wire, start with a length of wire that is as long as the length of the bead plus ³/₄" (1.9cm). For 18 gauge wire, use a length of wire that is as long as the length of the bead plus 1" (2.5cm).

Here is a selection of bead links with wrapped loops ready for use in a project. To make a bead link with a wrapped loop at each end, cut a length of 20 gauge wire that is as long as the length of the bead plus 2" (5.1cm). Make a wrapped loop at one end of the wire, string on the bead, then make a wrapped loop in the remaining end.

Bead Drops

This bead drop started with a plain loop at one end. Next, a bead was added and the wire was formed into a small curl under the bead. This is just one way to make a drop.

These drops all began with a wrapped loop and were finished in various ways. To finish a drop, the wire end can be formed into a loop, coiled up to the bead, hammered until the bead stays in place, or hammered and then coiled around the bead. If you'd like to make a coiled end like the drop with the blue bead above, see the instructions below. A simple hammered end like the drop on the left requires only $1/8"$–$1/4"$ (3mm–6mm) of wire, while wrapping around the bead may take 1" (2.5cm) of wire or more.

Coiled End

Coiling is basic to wire jewelry. Flat coils are a neat way to finish the ends of wires, and are commonly used in filigree work. You can use this technique to make open or closed coils—open coils have gaps between the rounds.

1 Grasp the end of the wire in a pair of round nose pliers and turn the pliers away from yourself until a complete loop forms. If a tiny loop is needed, use the tips of the round nose pliers.

2 Grasp the loop with flat nose pliers; bring the wire around the center loop. Reposition the pliers and continue turning as needed until the coil is the size you desire. Leave slight gaps between the rounds if making an open coil.

Jump Rings

Jump rings are used to connect jewelry components. They can be opened and closed, so you can use them to connect pieces at any time in the assembly process. You can purchase or make jump rings.

Most of the jump rings used in this book are one of two sizes: the first size is a $3/16$" (5mm) jump ring with a $1/8$" (3mm) interior diameter made from 18 gauge wire (formed on a $1/8$" [3mm] dowel or the handle of a needle file); the other is a $3/8$" (1cm) jump ring with a $1/4$" (6mm) interior diameter made from 16 gauge wire (formed on a $1/4$" [6mm] dowel). Jump rings of other sizes may be made by using dowels of various sizes. Allow approximately 1" (2.5cm) of wire for a $1/4$" (6mm), 16 gauge jump ring, and $1/2$" (1.3cm) of wire for a $3/16$" (5mm), 18 gauge jump ring.

Using Pliers to Make Jump Rings

This method works well if you need only one or two jump rings. For making a larger quantity, however, it is slow and usually results in rings of unequal sizes. I recommend using the jeweler's saw method (see page 24) for making several jump rings at a time.

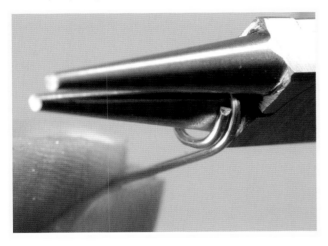

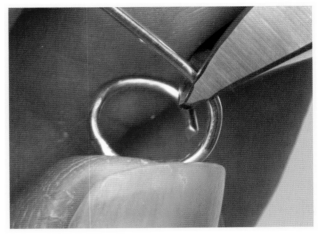

1 Grasp the end of the wire using a pair of round nose pliers. Pick the spot on the plier jaws that is as thick as you want the inner diameter of the jump ring to be. If you are making more than a single jump ring and want them to match, mark the exact place on the plier jaws with a scratch or a piece of masking tape. Turn the pliers away from yourself until a complete loop forms.

2 Swivel the ring open far enough to allow the wire to be cut with a pair of wire cutters. Using the cutters in the direction that will result in a flush cut, cut the wire at the overlap.

3 Use a bastard file to make each end of the ring perfectly flat.

Using a Jeweler's Saw to Make Jump Rings

Sawing coiled wire results in rings that are even in size with flat ends that will close neatly. Rings made using this method need little to no finishing because the saw cuts straight through the wire, making flat ends on both ends of the rings. You will need a jeweler's saw and a bench vise to make rings in this way.

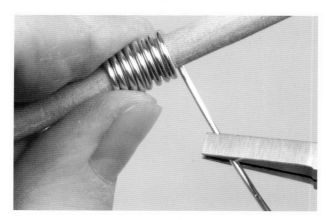

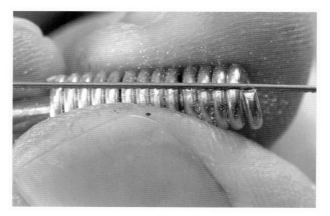

1 To begin, make a wire coil. Wrap the wire by hand or with a pair of flat nose pliers. As you wrap, pull on the wire and make the wraps close to each other. To make jump rings with a 1/4" (6mm) interior diameter from 16 gauge wire, use a 1/4" (6mm) dowel for both forming and sawing the rings. Form jump rings with a 1/8" (3mm) interior diameter made from 18 gauge wire on the handle of a needle file or on a 1/8" (3mm) dowel; place the coil on a 2 1/2" (6.4cm) long nail for sawing.

2 Place the dowel or nail into a bench vise at an angle. Place the wire coil on the end of the dowel or nail and hold on to it. Begin sawing very slowly to start a groove for the blade. Angle the saw so the blade cuts through the first ring while at the same time begins to cut into the next 2–3 rings. Keep your hand cupped under the coil to catch the rings as they fall.

Always saw with a slow and even motion and keep your eyes on your work. Cutting a finger on the saw can happen easily if you saw too fast or if your attention strays, so please be careful.

Opening and Closing Jump Rings

Use the method below to open and securely close jump rings that you've made or purchased.

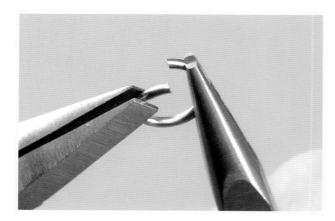

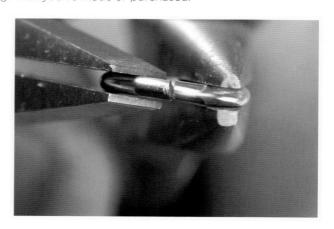

1 To open a jump ring, use a pair of chain nose pliers and a pair of flat nose pliers to grip the jump ring on either side of the cut. Swivel the ends away from each other.

2 To close a jump ring, swivel the ends back and forth several times—the ends should grate against each other as they pass. On the last pass, align the ends. The join should be barely perceptible.

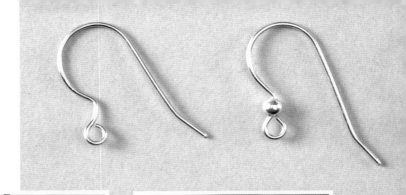

Ear Wires

It is easy and inexpensive to make your own ear wires. Use any alloy of gold or silver half-hard wire. (Avoid base metals as some can cause allergic reactions.) This basic ear wire is used in many of the earring designs in this book.

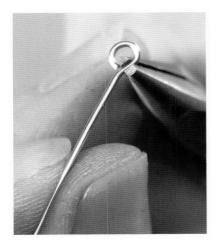

1 Cut 2¼" (5.7cm) of 20 gauge wire. Form a plain loop at one end of the wire (see Plain Loops on page 19).

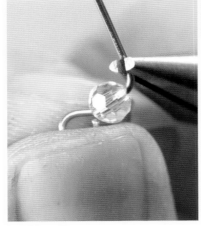

2 If you like, string a 3mm metal or crystal bead on the wire. Using a pair of chain nose pliers, bend the wire forward over the top of the bead (parallel with the beginning loop). If you don't use a bead, clamp a pair of chain nose pliers onto the wire above the plain loop and bend the wire forward over the pliers (again, parallel with the loop).

3 Shape the ear wire over a ³⁄₈" (1cm) dowel.

4 If you wish to, you can lightly hammer the area above the bead to flatten it up to where the wire will make contact with the ear.

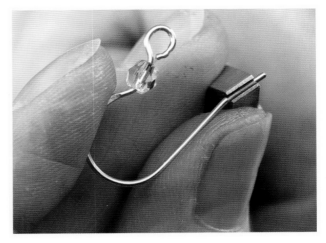

5 Use chain nose pliers to make a small outward bend about ³⁄₁₆" (5mm) from the wire end. Use a file or emery cloth to smooth the wire end.

Clasps

Clasps are a wonderful way to practice your wire working skills. They are small, so they don't take a lot of time, and you can keep your successes on hand to use in a future project. Several different kinds of clasps are used throughout the book and they are all outlined over the following pages.

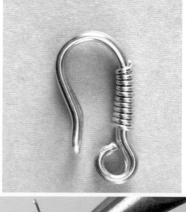

Hook Clasp

To make this clasp, a single length of wire is formed into a doubled hook. To close a bracelet or necklace, the hook is joined through a large loop. A hook clasp works well for bracelets that are fitted to the wrist. Make a fancy version by wrapping the clasp with 24 gauge wire.

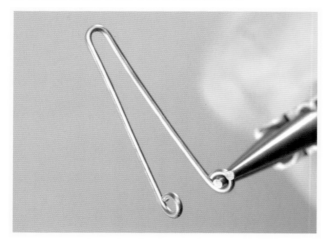

1 To make a clasp that is ⅝" (1.6cm) long, cut a 3" (7.6cm) length of 18 gauge round wire. (Adjust the length of the wire to make a clasp of a different size.) Grasp the wire at the center using a pair of round nose pliers and bend it in half. Use round nose pliers to form a loop on each end (see Plain Loops on page 19). Make the loops the correct size to join them to your jewelry piece.

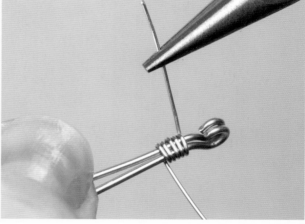

2 If you'd like your clasp to be more decorative, use 3" (7.6cm) of 24 gauge wire to wrap the clasp close to the end loops. Hammer lightly to set the wraps.

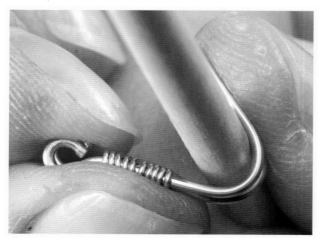

3 Form the doubled wire into a hook by bending it over a ³⁄₁₆" (5mm) dowel.

4 With the clasp still on the dowel, use a pair of flat nose pliers to bend the end of the hook slightly upward.

S Clasp

The S clasp is a multipurpose clasp that is attractive and simple to make. To connect a necklace or bracelet, each end is hooked through a loop. It works very well for necklaces.

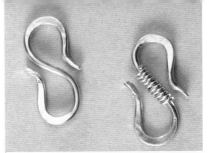

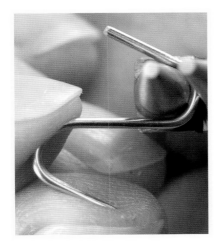

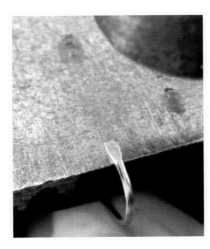

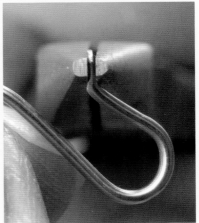

1 To make a clasp that is ⁵/₈" (1.6cm) long, cut a 1¹/₂" (3.8cm) length of 18 gauge round wire. (Adjust the length of the wire to make a clasp of a different size.) Using a pair of round nose pliers, grasp the wire near the widest part of the jaw ¹/₂" (1.3cm) from one end of the wire. Bend both ends of the wire to form a U shape over the jaw of the pliers. Do the same at the other end to bend it in the opposite direction.

2 Holding the shaped wire vertically, hammer ¹/₈" (3mm) of each end to flatten them.

3 Use a pair of chain nose pliers to bend each end slightly outward.

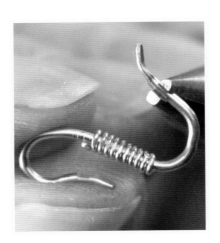

4 To make a decorative clasp, use 2" (5.1cm) of 24 gauge wire to wrap the center of the clasp.

5 Position the ends close to the center and across from each other.

6 As a finishing touch, hammer the outer parts of the clasp, avoiding the center and the hammered ends.

Toggle Clasp

The toggle clasp is made up of two pieces: a crossbar and a loop. It is an ideal closure for many bracelet styles. You can adjust the length of the jump ring chains that attach the clasp to the piece of jewelry to achieve a perfect fit.

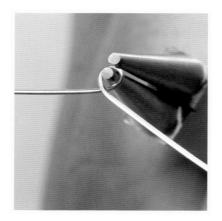

1 To make the bar of the toggle clasp, grasp the center of a 3½" (8.9cm) length of 22 gauge wire in the tips of a pair of round nose pliers. Cross the ends to form a small loop. This loop must be small so that the crossbar will fit easily through the loop of the clasp.

2 Straddle the loop over a ⅞" (2.2cm) length of 16 gauge wire. Bring the ends of the 22 gauge wire downward and cross the ends under the bar. Proceed to wrap first one end of the wire, then the other completely around the crossbar.

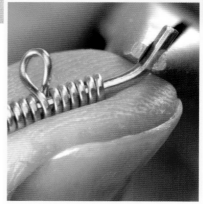

3 Give the loop a complete turn. Hammer the wraps lightly to settle them onto the bar. Use a pair of chain nose pliers to turn the ends of the bar upward slightly.

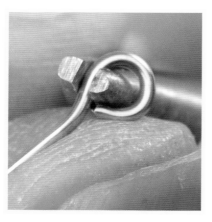

4 To make the loop portion of the clasp, form a small plain loop at one end of a 2½" (6.3cm) length of 20 gauge wire (see Plain Loops on page 19).

5 Grasp the wire with a pair of chain nose pliers just beneath the loop; push the wire end to the side to form a 90 degree angle.

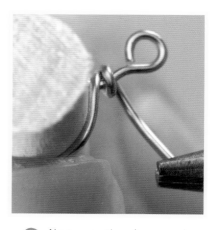

6 Next, wrap the wire around a 5⁄16" (8mm) dowel to form a large loop. Keep the loop on the dowel and wrap the wire end to fill in the gap between the large and small loops. Add jump rings onto the small loops on the crossbar and the loop sections of the clasp.

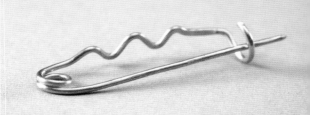

Pin Back

A pin back is a finding that is sewn or wired onto the back of a piece of jewelry to make the jewelry wearable as a brooch. The zigzag shape helps to keep the pin back in place once it is wired on. The instructions given below are for a pin back that is 1¼" (3.2cm) long. For other sizes, use more or less wire as needed.

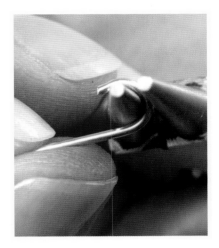

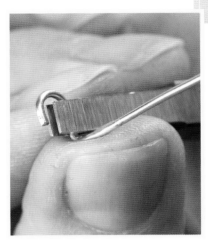

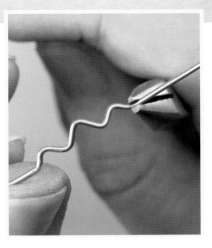

1 Cut 5" (12.7cm) of 18 gauge wire. Use round nose pliers to bend one end into a U shape. (This will serve as the catch for the pin.)

2 Grasp the catch with a pair of chain nose pliers or flat nose pliers and bend the end upward at a 90 degree angle.

3 Working from the angle just made, and using the tip of the chain nose pliers, bend the wire several times to make a zigzag. The zigzag section should be 1¼" (3.2cm) long. Lightly hammer the zigzag section to flatten it.

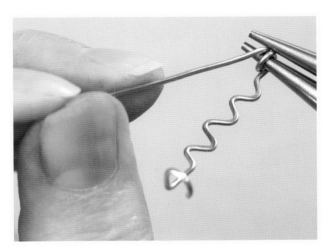

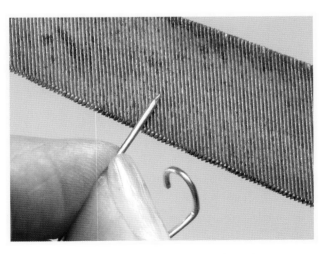

4 Clamp a pair of round nose pliers on the wire 1¼" (3.2cm) from the catch; bring the wire around to form a complete circle. The end of the wire should now be pointing back toward the catch.

5 Close the pin and trim the wire ¼" (6mm) beyond the catch. Open the pin and lightly hammer the entire pin section to harden the metal. While you are hammering, continually turn the piece on the anvil to hammer evenly. Use a bastard file to taper the pin end. Lightly round the end so it is not sharp.

Bead Strands

I like to use bead strands for the backs of necklaces to make them more comfortable to wear—if the back of a necklace is made from wire, it can catch in the wearer's hair. Beads also add color and variety to a piece. To create a bead strand you'll need beads, wrapped bead links (see page 21), beading wire and crimp beads. Beading wire consists of fine strands of wire encased in a nylon coating. This type of wire is available in various colors, sizes, strengths and amounts of flexibility. I recommend keeping a variety of sizes on hand to fit beads with holes of different sizes (the bead hole must accommodate two thicknesses of beading wire). Crimp beads are used to secure the ends of the bead strand. Crimp beads are available in a range of sizes—purchase crimp beads in sizes that match your beading wires (a crimp bead must be large enough to accommodate two thicknesses of beading wire).

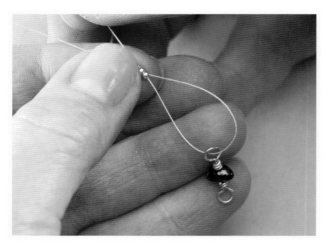

1 Cut a length of beading wire that equals the desired length of the finished bead strand plus at least 6" (15.2cm). String a crimp bead, then a wrapped bead link onto the bead wire. Run about 3" (7.6cm) of the beading wire back through the crimp bead.

2 Arrange the wires so they lie side by side inside the crimp bead. Using the back section of a pair of crimping pliers, clamp onto the crimp bead and squeeze. This separates the wires inside the crimp bead.

Place the crimp bead into the front section of the crimping pliers with a crimped wire in the upper rounded area and the other in the bottom. Squeeze the pliers closed. This brings the halves of the crimp bead together, rounding it.

3 String the beads for the strand onto the beading wire, sliding them onto the doubled wire at the finished end. Continue stringing beads and once the desired length has been strung, string a crimp bead and a bead link onto the wire. Bring the end of the wire through the crimp bead again. String the wire through about 1" (2.5cm) of beads, then bring the wire out to the side of the strand. Pull on the wire to settle everything into place, then finish the crimp bead as before. Trim off the excess bead wire.

Twisted Wire

Using twisted wire is one easy way to add an extra visual punch to a project. A single length of square wire can be twisted alone; the corners of the wire will then catch the light and add interest to your jewelry piece. You can also twist two or more lengths of wire together. Twisting wires of the same color will add texture to a piece while twisting wires of different colors together can take color play to a whole new level in your jewelry.

1 First, clamp the wire or wires into a bench vise. Clean the wire with a rouge cloth. If you are twisting 2 or more lengths of wire together, check that they are parallel to each other. Fasten the remaining wire end into the jaws of the twisting device.

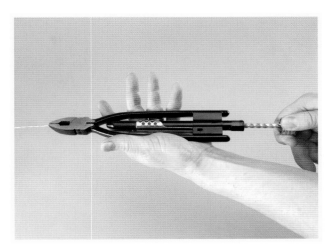

2 Stand back so the wires is taut. Squeeze the handles of the device until the catch engages, then slide the catch back to hold the pliers in a locked position. Hold the handles in one hand, and pull back on the rounded button at the end with the other hand. Let go of the button and let the tool twist. Repeat until the wire has the amount of twist you desire, or until the wire snaps apart from the vise. Squeeze the handles of the tool to release the wire.

About the Projects

Now that we have covered the techniques you'll need to get started, we can dive into the projects. In some of the following step-by-step photos, the wire and/or beads do not match the finished piece. Because the photography for a book of this kind requires the creation of many projects in progress, inexpensive brass wire was used to demonstrate the project steps.

hammered wire

I f you are new to jewelry making or to wire working, I suggest starting with the projects in this chapter. Hammering is a simple technique, but you can still use it to create beautiful jewelry. Hammering wire not only changes the look of the wire, it work hardens the metal at the same time. This work hardening allows you to create pieces that appear more delicate than they actually are. The subtle texture hammering provides allows light to play off the wire in various ways. The real beauty of the hammered wire technique is that designs can be very simple in their structure and yet have a wonderful, timeless air of sophistication—your jewelry will never go out of style.

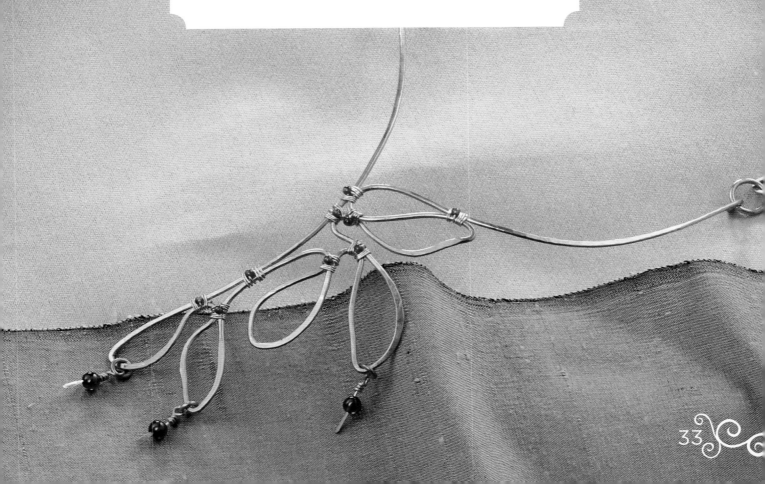

Embedded Coils Necklace

This is perhaps the simplest project in this book, and because it takes a personal touch, no two can ever be alike! Practice your hammering technique to make the coils, then mesh them together. Since this design is a mix of two metals you can make the pendant, clasp and bead links out of either metal.

Finished Size: approx. 20" (50.8cm) long

materials list

18" (45.7cm) of 18 gauge round wire

9" (22.9cm) of 18 gauge round wire in a different metal or color

12½" (31.8cm) of 22 gauge round wire

16" (40.6cm) strand of 6mm round verdite beads

12mm round verdite bead

5 jump rings—³⁄₈" (1cm), 16 gauge (see pages 23–24 to make your own)

S clasp (see page 27 to make your own)

Beading wire

4 crimp beads

½" (1.3cm) dowel

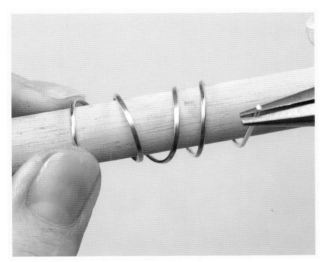

1 Cut 9" (22.9cm) of 18 gauge wire. Holding the wire firmly to prevent it from rotating, hammer the entire length to flatten the wire (see Hammering on page 18). The wire will naturally begin to curl. Place the center of the hammered wire against a ½" (1.3cm) dowel and coil it around the dowel in the direction of the curl established by hammering. Leave 1" (2.5cm) at each end uncoiled.

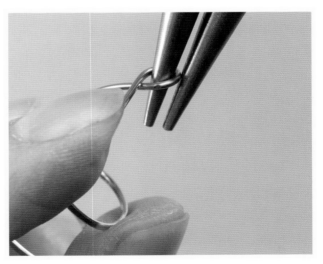

2 Grasp the coiled wire 1" (2.5cm) from the end with a pair of round nose pliers and turn the pliers away from you to form a complete loop.

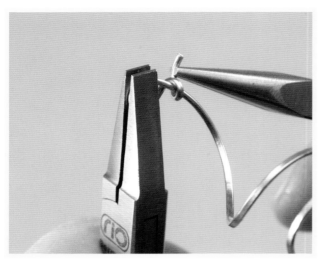

3 Grasp the loop with flat nose pliers and use chain nose pliers to wrap the wire end beneath the loop (see Wrapped Loops on page 20). Repeat at the other end.

4 Hold the wire at each end and stretch it widthwise until it is about 3¹/₂" (8.9cm) long. Bring the ends upward to form a slight U shape.

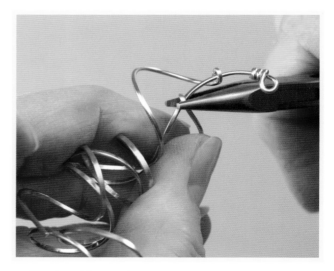

5 Cut 9" (22.9cm) of 18 gauge wire and repeat Step 1. Make each of the coils in this and the following steps slightly uneven for a natural look. Stretching to fit, mesh this wire into the coil made earlier. Fasten the second coil onto the first with a tight loop at each end directly below the wrapped loops (see Tight Loops on page 21).

6 Cut 6" (15.2cm) of 18 gauge wire in a different metal or color; hammer, coil and shape this wire like the others. Mesh the new coil with the others, centering it within the coils. Fasten with tight loops at each end onto any convenient wire.

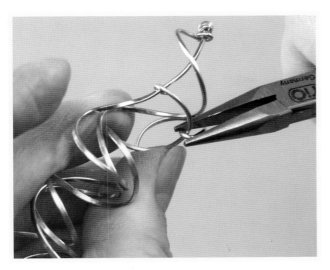

7 Repeat Step 6 using 3" (7.6cm) of 18 gauge wire in a different metal or color.

8 Cut 3½" (8.9cm) of 22 gauge wire and make a wrapped loop at one end. String on a 6mm verdite bead followed by a 12mm verdite bead. Hammer the wire end up to the beads to flatten. Leaving a slight gap between the beads, bend the wire sharply upward under the 12mm bead, curl it around the bead, and fasten with a tight loop between the beads. Fasten the drop onto the center of the meshed coils using a ³⁄₈" (1cm) jump ring.

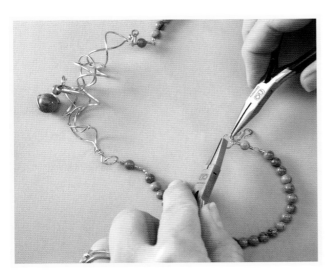

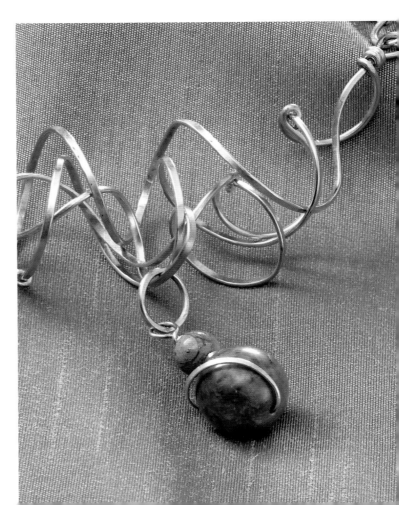

9 Make 4 wrapped bead links—use 2¼" (5.7cm) of 22 gauge wire and 1 verdite bead for each (see Bead Links on page 21). Make 2 strands of 6mm verdite beads, each 6" (15.2cm) long, with a wrapped bead link at each end (see Bead Strands on page 30). Place a ³⁄₈" (1cm) jump ring on each end of each strand. Fasten a bead strand to each end of the meshed coils. Close the necklace with an S clasp.

Hammered Rings Necklace

In this necklace, hammered and wrapped rings are assembled into a continuous round, then doubled and attached to a bead strand for the back of the necklace. Stagger the strands of rings simply by choosing where to fasten the clasp. If you like, you can make this necklace longer by adding additional hammered rings and jump rings.

Finished Size: approx. 16"–18" (40.6cm–45.7cm) long depending on how it is worn

materials list

60" (152.4cm) of 18 gauge round wire

54" (137.2cm) of 24 gauge round wire

22½" (57.2cm) of 22 gauge round wire

16" (40.6cm) strand of 6mm round old crazy lace agate beads

48 jump rings—³⁄₈" (1cm), 16 gauge (see pages 23–24 to make your own)

11 jump rings—³⁄₁₆" (5mm), 18 gauge (see pages 23–24 to make your own)

S clasp (see page 27 to make your own)

Beading wire

2 crimp beads

½" (1.3cm) dowel

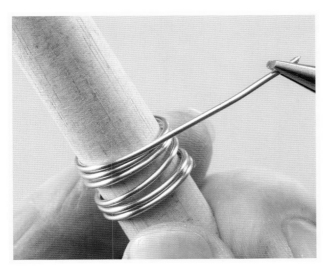

1 To make the hammered rings, begin by wrapping 60" (152.4cm) of 18 gauge wire around a ½" (1.3cm) dowel. Wrap snugly and keep the wraps close together. Remove the coiled wire from the dowel.

2 Pull the loops apart a bit and begin cutting the rings using a pair of side cutters. Cut each ring to include a ½" (1.3cm) overlap.

3 Placing one end inside the other, hammer each ring individually to flatten the wire (see Hammering on page 18).

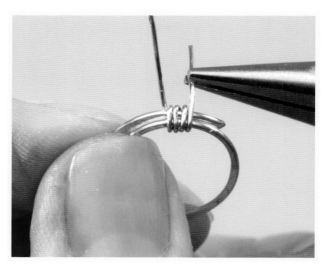

4 Cut a 2¼" (5.7cm) length of 24 gauge wire for each ring. Keeping one end inside the other, wrap the 24 gauge wire around the center of the overlap (see Wrapping on page 17). To set the wraps, hammer them lightly.

5 Hammer each ³/₈" (1cm) jump ring to lightly flatten the ring.

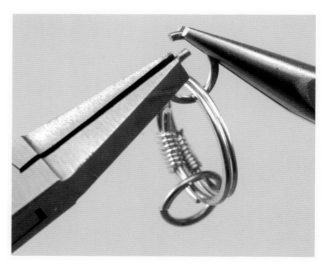

6 Assemble the rings and jump rings. Start by opening 2 of the ³/₈" (1cm) jump rings. Hold 2 of the hammered, wrapped rings together and fasten 2 jump rings, 1 at a time, onto the pair of hammered, wrapped rings. Bring the 2 jump rings together and separate the 2 hammered, wrapped rings so that the piece now looks like 2 hammered, wrapped rings connected side-by-side by 2 jump rings. Continue to assemble the chain by connecting a single hammered, wrapped ring to the chain with a pair of jump rings. Continue until all rings are used. Join the ends of the chain with 2 jump rings to form a closed circle.

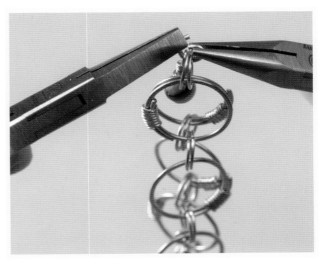

7 Make 9 wrapped bead drops using 2" (5.1cm) of 22 gauge wire and a single 6mm bead for each (see Bead Drops on page 22). Form a wrapped loop in one end, string on a 6mm bead, hammer the wire end, then curl it up and over the bead and fasten with a tight loop above the bead.

8 Use a ³/₁₆" (5mm) jump ring to fasten a bead drop onto any pair of ³/₈" (1cm) jump rings. Place the remaining bead drops randomly the same way.

9 Make 2 wrapped bead links—use 2¼" (5.7cm) of 22 gauge wire and 1 old crazy lace agate bead for each (see Bead Links on page 21). Make a 4½" (11.4cm) strand of 6mm old crazy lace agate beads with a wrapped bead link at each end (see Bead Strands on page 30). Fasten the end of the strand to any hammered, wrapped loop with a pair of ³/₁₆" (5mm) jump rings. Fasten a ³/₈" (1cm) jump ring to the other end of the bead strand. Join the necklace with an S clasp through the ³/₈" (1cm) jump ring and any hammered, wrapped ring.

Artifact in Three Metals

For me, this bracelet design evokes images of fine pieces of jewelry that have been unearthed in archaeological digs. It has the character of ancient jewelry created during the time when fine wires were first being used to form adornments. The lepidolite bead adds to this look. I've made this in three different metals to show the marvelous versatility of this design.

Finished Size: approx. 7¹/₂" (19cm) long (including clasp)

materials list

15" (38.1cm) of 18 gauge round wire

12" (30.5cm) of 22 gauge round wire

14mm × 11mm flat rectangular lepidolite bead

Toggle clasp (see page 28 to make your own)

Permanent marker

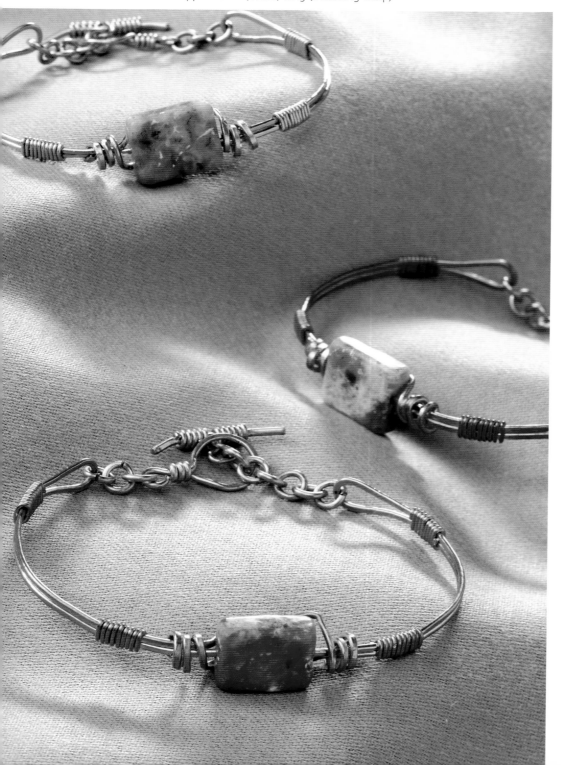

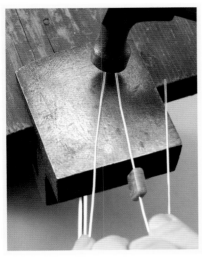

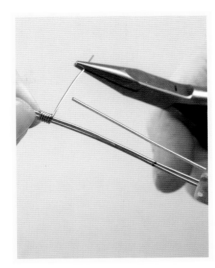

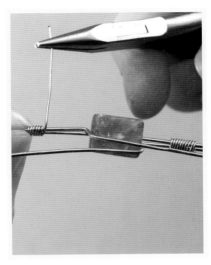

1 Mark the center of a 15" (38.1cm) length of 18 gauge wire with a permanent marker. Mark 2³/₄" (7cm) away from the center in each direction as well. Using round nose pliers, bend one side of the wire at the 2³/₄" (7cm) mark into a U shape. Place the bead onto the longer end of the wire, then bend the wire in the opposite direction at the other 2³/₄" (7cm) mark. Hammer the entire piece to flatten the wire, moving the bead aside as needed (see Hammering on page 18).

2 Use a permanent marker to make four more marks: Mark ⁵/₈" (1.6cm) and 2" (5.1cm) in from each end of the folded wire. Cut 3" (7.6cm) of 22 gauge wire and use the wire to make a wrap centered on a ⁵/₈" (1.6cm) mark, bringing the two wires together (see Wrapping on page 17). Repeat on the other end of the bracelet.

3 Center the bead on the wire. Mold each loose wire end to fit over the back of the bead; bend the wire with sharp angles to fit the shape of the rectangular bead. Make a wrap around the two main wires (not the loose ends) using 3" (7.6cm) of 22 gauge wire at each of the 2" (5.1cm) marks made in the previous step.

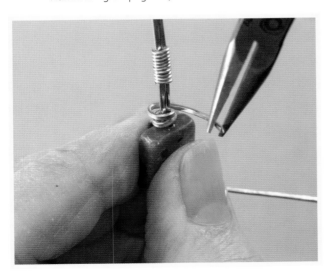

4 Bring a loose wire end up at the end of the bead and loosely wrap it alongside the bead. Repeat for the other loose wire end.

5 Form the bracelet into a rounded shape over a mandrel or dowel to shape it to fit your wrist. Fasten on a toggle clasp.

Sculpted Leaves Neckpiece

Tiny garnets and wraps made from fine wire distinguish this shaped piece. Practice your wire shaping skills to form the leaves, then wrap on garnets for flashes of color. A doubled strand of fine beads forms the back of the necklace.

Finished Size: fits like a 16" (40.6cm) necklace

materials list

27" (68.6cm) of 16 gauge round wire

22¹/₂" (57.2cm) of 26 gauge round wire

9" (22.9cm) of 22 gauge round wire

6" (15.2cm) strand of 4mm round garnet beads

10" (25.4cm) strand of 2mm round garnet beads

1 jump ring—³/₈" (1cm), 16 gauge (see pages 23–24 to make your own)

3 jump rings—³/₁₆" (5mm), 18 gauge (see pages 23–24 to make your own)

S clasp (see page 27 to make your own)

Beading wire

4 crimp beads

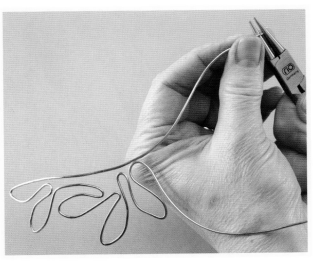

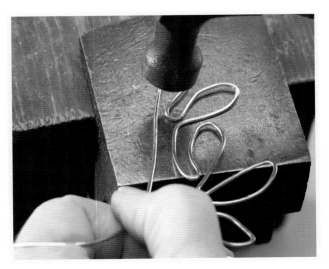

1 Grasp the end of a 27" (68.6cm) length of 16 gauge wire with a pair of round nose pliers. Turn the pliers away from yourself to form a complete loop. Beginning at one end of the template on page 47, form the entire neckpiece. Use a pair of pliers as needed, but form the wire by hand where possible. At the other end, trim off any excess wire using a pair of side cutters. Form a loop in this end to match the first end.

2 With the wrong side of the piece facing up, hammer the wire except for the last 2" (5.1cm) of each end (see Hammering on page 18). Stop periodically to check the shape of the wire against the diagram; reshape as needed. Hammer more heavily in some areas than others to create a forged look.

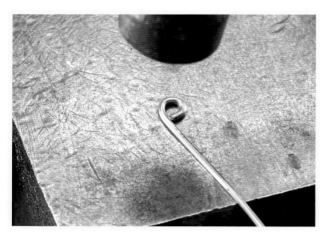

3 Turn the wire onto its side to hammer each of the ends, including the end loops.

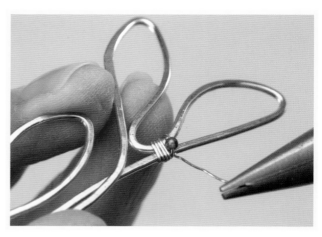

4 Cut 9 lengths of 26 gauge wire, each 2½" (6.4cm) long. Use these wires to wrap the neckpiece at each place where 2 wires touch. To make the wraps, center the 26 gauge wire on the area to be wrapped and make the first half of the wrap (see Wrapping on page 17). String a 2mm garnet bead on the wire, then make the second half of the wrap.

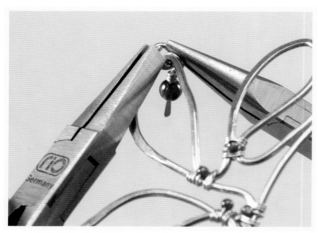

5 Make 3 wrapped bead drops with hammered ends; use 1½" (3.8cm) of 22 gauge wire and a 4mm garnet bead for each (see Bead Drops on page 22). Hammer the unwrapped end of the drop to secure the bead on the wire. Attach the drops to leaves on the neckpiece using a ³⁄₁₆" (5mm) jump ring for each.

6 Make 2 wrapped bead links—use 2¼" (5.7cm) of 22 gauge wire and a 4mm garnet bead for each (see Bead Links on page 21). Make 2 garnet bead strands, each 7" (17.8cm) long (see Bead Strands on page 30). Begin by attaching both strands of beading wire to the same wrapped bead link, then string beads on each strand in the following order: begin with 3 garnet 4mm beads, alternate 6 garnet 2mm beads with 1 garnet 4mm bead until the strand measures 6½" (16.5cm), then end with 3 garnet 4mm beads. Attach both strands to the second wrapped bead link. Fasten a bead link to an end loop of the hammered wire. Place a ³⁄₈" (1cm) jump ring onto the other end of the hammered piece and use an S clasp to join the necklace. Try on the neckpiece; if needed, gently shape the hammered piece to fit comfortably.

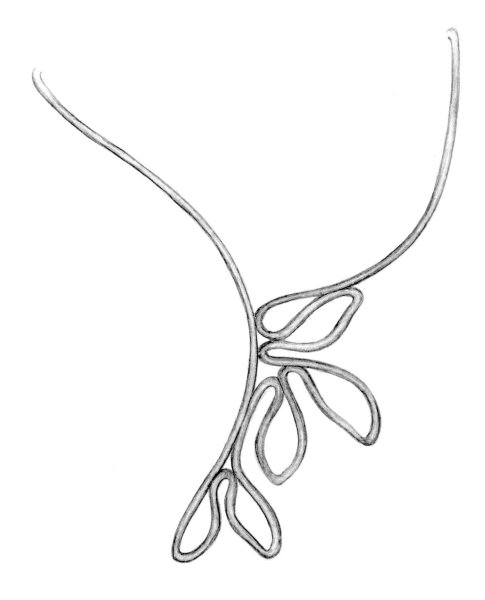

Trio of Hammered Wire Earrings

Make this set of earrings for some variety in your earring collection. The simple-to-make Open Leaf earring on page 49 is made from one piece of wire and a series of bends. For variety, try them in different metals. In the Floating Spiral on page 50, an encircling wire holds a bead in its midst. The Nautilus earring on page 52 is a wearable sculpture, sure to elicit compliments. The need for artful shaping of the wires makes this a project for the more experienced wire worker. Work one in practice wire first, then make both earrings at the same time so they come out as a matching set.

Finished Size: Open Leaf, approx. 2¼" (5.7cm) long × ½" (1.3cm) wide; Floating Spiral, approx. 1" (2.5cm) long × ⅝" (1.6cm) wide; Nautilus, approx. 1" (2.5cm) long × 1⅛" (2.9cm) wide

materials list

OPEN LEAF
16" (40.6cm) of 20 gauge round wire

Ear wires (see page 25 to make your own)

Note: Because these are long earrings, I recommend making a short ear wire using 2" (5.1cm) of 20 gauge wire.

Permanent marker

Painter's tape

FLOATING SPIRAL
3¾" (9.5cm) of 18 gauge round wire

24" (61cm) of 20 gauge round wire

2 porcelain oval beads, each 9mm wide × 15mm long

Ear wires

½" (1.3cm) dowel

NAUTILUS
12" (30.5cm) of 18 gauge round wire

36" (91.4cm) of 20 gauge round wire

Ear wires with a 3mm pearl

⅜" (1cm) dowel

5/16" (8mm) dowel

¼" (6mm) dowel

3/16" (5mm) dowel

Open Leaf

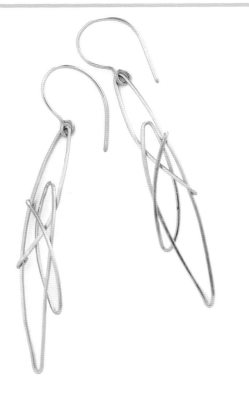

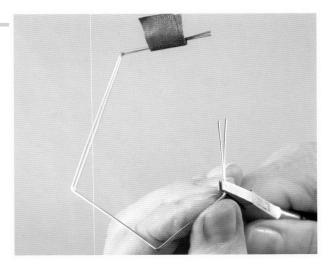

1 Cut 2 lengths of 20 gauge wire, each 8" (20.3cm) long. Tape them together near one end with painter's tape. Using a ruler and permanent marker, mark 1½" (3.8cm) from the taped end. Mark again at 3¾" (9.5cm) from the taped end, then 5½" (14cm) from the taped end, then 6¾" (17.1cm) from the taped end. Use a pair of flat nose pliers to make a sharp bend at each mark; make all bends in the same direction.

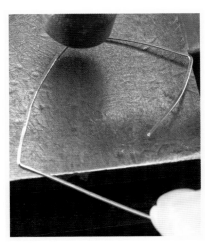

2 Remove the tape; from here on work each wire separately. Hammer each wire entirely, except for the last ¼" (6mm) of each end (see Hammering on page 18). Using chain nose pliers, work along each section between bends, gently bending each into a slight curve. When you shape the second wire, make it a mirror image of the first.

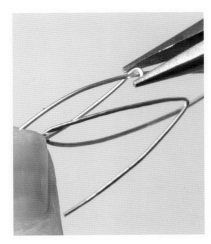

3 As you shape the wire, bring the segments closer together. Weave the beginning 1½" (3.8cm) section under, then over the smaller, final section. Fasten the end of the 1½" (3.8cm) section with a tight loop onto the second section (see Tight Loops on page 21).

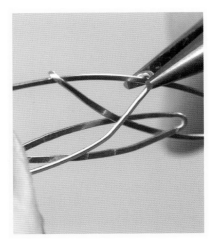

4 Bring the final end over all segments, then fasten it with a tight loop onto the same section with the previous connection. Fasten an ear wire to the top of the shaped wire. Repeat Steps 3–4 on the second earring.

Floating Spiral

1 Cut 12" (30.5cm) of 20 gauge round wire. Use a pair of round nose pliers to form a small loop in one end (use the tips of the pliers to make the smallest loop). Change to a pair of flat nose pliers and coil the wire around the small loop until the flat coil has four complete rounds (see Coiled End on page 22). Repeat at the other end of the wire, making this coil in the opposite direction.

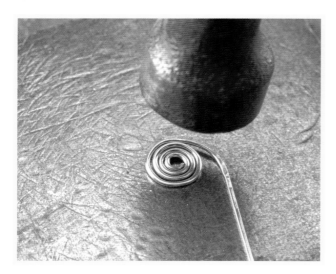

2 Hammer the entire piece to flatten slightly (see Hammering on page 18).

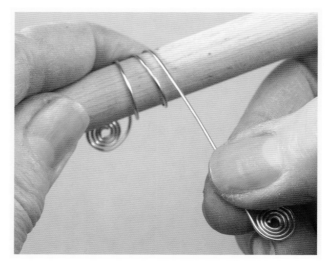

3 Place the center of the wire over a ¹/₂" (1.3cm) dowel and wrap each end around the dowel up to the flat coil at each end.

4 Remove the wire from the dowel and bend each flat coil inward to form the bead cage.

5 Insert the bead into the bead cage by moving the coils apart.

6 Cut a 1⁷/₈" (4.8cm) length of 18 gauge wire. Run the 18 gauge wire through the centers of the flat coils of the bead cage and the hole of the bead. Dome each wire coil by pressing it against the bead.

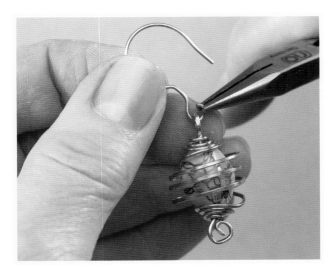

7 Form one end of the 18 gauge wire into a plain loop centered over the bead (see Plain Loops on page 19). Hammer the remaining end of the wire and curl it up to the bead. If needed, arrange the bead cage so the coils do not touch the bead. Place an ear wire on the plain loop. Make a second earring in the same way.

Nautilus

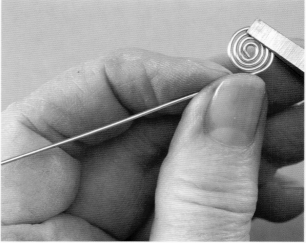

1 Cut a 6" (15.2cm) length of 18 gauge round wire. Use a pair of round nose pliers to form a small loop in one end (use the tips of the pliers to make the smallest loop). Change to a pair of flat nose pliers and coil the wire around the small loop until the flat coil has four complete rounds (see Coiled End on page 22).

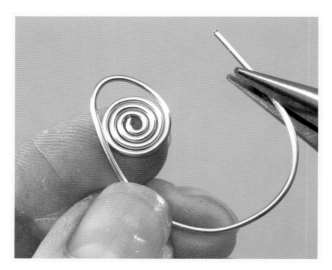

2 Use chain nose pliers to bend the wire upward from the coil to form a hanging loop, then bend the wire downward and curve the end. Hammer the wire to flatten it (see Hammering on page 18).

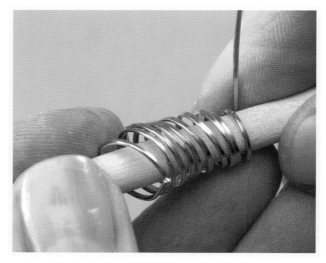

3 Cut 18" (45.7cm) of 20 gauge wire. Hammer the entire length flat without rotating the wire. Beginning at one end of the wire, wrap it around a ³/₈" (1cm) dowel 5 times. Wrap the wire 5 times around a ⁵/₁₆" (8mm) dowel, directly next to the ³/₈" (1cm) wraps. Next, make 5 wraps around a ¹/₄" (6mm) dowel, then wrap the remaining wire around a ³/₁₆" (5mm) dowel. Try to make smooth transitions between the dowel sizes.

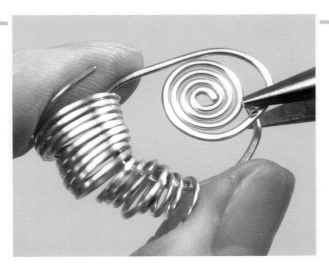

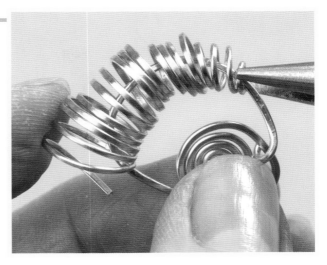

4 Place the spiralled wire, wide end first, onto the uncoiled end of the frame created in Steps 1–2. Bring the frame wire end upward in a smooth curve. Fasten the end with a tight loop onto the hanging loop just above the flat coil (see Tight Loops on page 21).

5 Fasten the small end of the spiral with a tight loop onto the wire frame.

6 Fasten the wide end of the spiral with a tight loop onto the wire frame. Trim the wire if needed so that the topmost coil retains its open shape. Arrange the wraps of the spiral artfully (and evenly spaced) along the frame. Add an ear wire to the hanging loop. Make a second earring that is the mirror image of the first.

Shadow Pavé Earrings

Create a pavé effect by sewing crystal beads onto a hammered wire base. The crystals glitter as they catch the light. I love the look of these shadowy crystal beads, but you can choose any color to customize your pair of earrings.

Finished Size: approx. 1³/₈" (3.5cm) long × 1" (2.5cm) wide

materials list

18" (45.7cm) of 18 gauge round wire

60" (152.4cm) of 26 gauge round wire

12" (30.5cm) strand of round glass or crystal 3mm beads in Montana Blue

2 round glass or crystal 4mm beads in Crystal

Ear wires (see page 25 to make your own)

1 Cut a 9" (22.9cm) length of 18 gauge wire. Grasp the end of the wire in the tips of a pair of round nose pliers and form a small loop. Change to flat nose pliers and make an open, flat coil by coiling 3 times around the center loop. Hammer the entire piece to flatten (see Hammering on page 18).

2 Cut a 30" (76.2cm) length of 26 gauge wire; fasten the wire onto the center of the coil just past the beginning loop with a few wraps (see Wrapping on page 17). String a 3mm bead onto the wire; thread the wire through the coil to the back. Going around the same round of the coil, bring the wire back up to the front. Continue sewing on beads in this manner until one round is complete. Continue sewing beads onto the second and third rounds, but also sew back into the previous round every 3–4 beads. This secures each round of the coil to another. After all 3 rounds are beaded, sew the 26 gauge wire back to the center of the coil. String a 4mm clear bead onto the wire, then wrap the wire 2–3 times around the center of the hammered coil to finish off.

3 Using a pair of round nose pliers, grasp the unbeaded 18 gauge wire ⅝" (1.6cm) away from the final bead; form a loop over the jaw of the pliers. Gently bend the wire end back toward the beaded coil, trim as needed, and fasten the end of the wire onto the coil with a tight loop between beads (see Tight Loops on page 21). Place an ear wire onto the loop. Repeat Steps 1–3 to make a second earring, mirroring the coil direction of the first earring for the second.

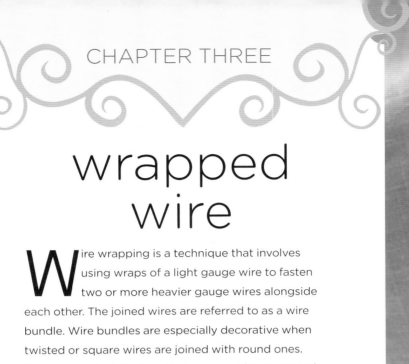

wrapped wire

Wire wrapping is a technique that involves using wraps of a light gauge wire to fasten two or more heavier gauge wires alongside each other. The joined wires are referred to as a wire bundle. Wire bundles are especially decorative when twisted or square wires are joined with round ones. Once connected, the bundled wires can be separated out and fastened independently in the design, creating opportunities for setting cabochons, creating bails, and fashioning decorative ends for bracelets and necklaces.

Waves & Wraps Bracelet

A single continuous wire wraps this bracelet from one end to the other. The wires are formed into curves and waves between wraps. You can widen this bracelet if you desire, but feel free to skip the extra wires, especially if you're a beginner.

Finished Size: approx. 6³/₄" (17.1cm) long without clasp

materials list

52" (132.1cm) of 20 gauge round wire

48" (121.9cm) of 22 gauge round wire

Toggle clasp (see page 28 to make your own)

Painter's tape

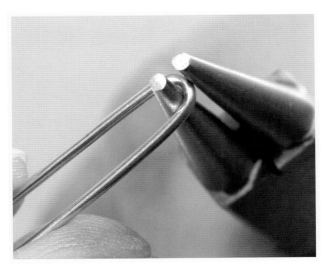

1 Cut 2 lengths of 20 gauge wire, each 18" (45.7cm) long. Grasp the center of the first wire with round nose pliers and bend it to form a U shape.

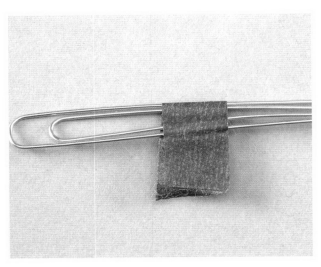

2 Repeat with the second wire, but make the second U wider than the first. Position the wires so that the narrow U is inside the wide U, and about ¹/₄" (6mm) lower. Tape the wires to hold them together.

Throughout the following steps, keep the 20 gauge wires parallel and lying flat.

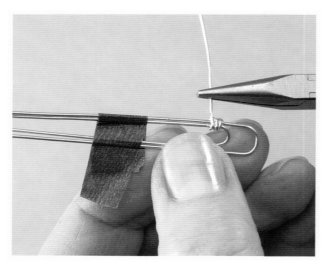

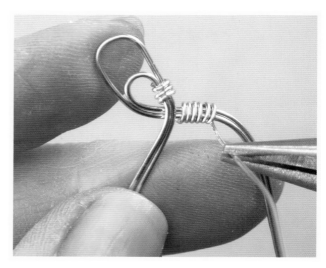

3 Wrap the end of a 48" (121.9cm) length of 22 gauge wire 3 times around the side of the piece formed in Step 2, near the bend in the narrow U (see Wrapping on page 17).

Hereafter, make all of the small wraps by wrapping 3 times.

4 Remove the tape from the wires. The wrapping wire should be to the back of the piece; if it is not, move it to the back. By hand, and moving 1 wire at a time, cross the left-hand 20 gauge wires under the right-hand ones while crossing the right-hand wires to the left. Bend a slight curve in the wires that are now on the right. Bring the wrapping wire up from the back and wrap the curved section for ⁵/₈" (1.6cm).

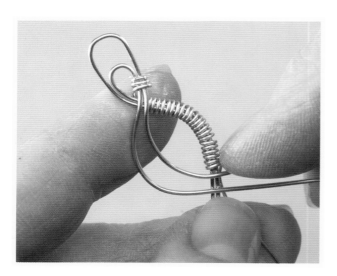

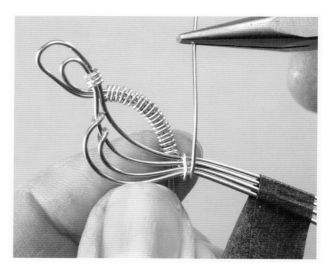

5 Form the wires on the left into an open swirl, crossing over the right-hand wires just beneath the wrapped section.

Throughout, keep the swirled wires to the front of the piece and the wrapped wires to the back.

6 Cut 2 lengths of 20 gauge wire, each 8" (20.3cm) long. Fasten each with a tight loop near the top of the swirl made in Step 5 (see Tight Loops on page 21). Swirl these wires to the right, arranging them alongside the previous swirled wires. Tape all 4 swirl wires together. Bring the wrapping wire under, then over the 4 wires. Make 3 wraps on the front, ending with the wrapping wire to the back.

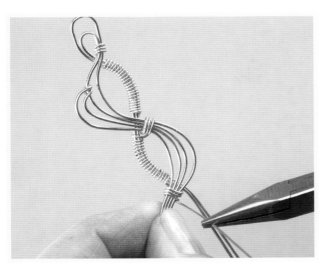

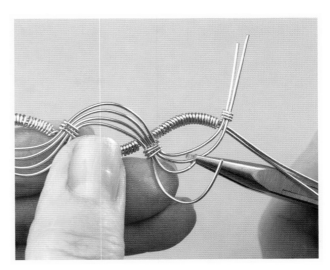

7 Bend a slight curve in the 2 wires that are now on the left. Bring the wrapping wire up from the back and wrap the curved section for ⅝" (1.6cm). Swirl the 4 right-hand wires, bringing them together directly after the wrapped section on the left wires. Use the wrapping wire to wrap the swirl wires 3 times. Continue in this manner until there are 7 wrapped 2-wire sections and 6 swirled 4-wire sections.

8 After the seventh wrapped section has been wrapped, swirl the inner 2 swirl wires. Fasten these 2 wires with 3 wraps, then end off the wrapping wire. Fasten each of the 2 loose swirl wires with a tight loop to the outer secured swirl wire.

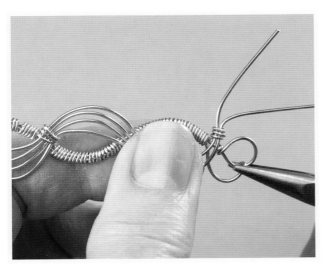

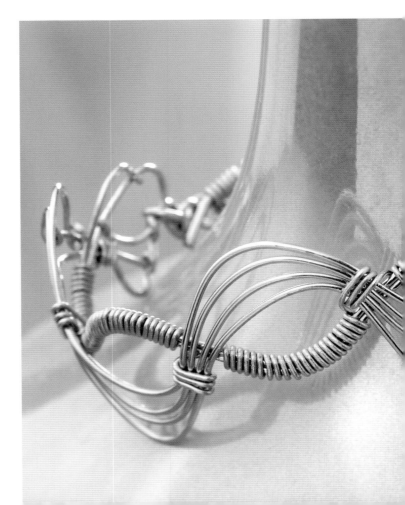

9 Use the innermost wrapped wire to form a wrapped loop ⅜" (1cm) in diameter from (see Wrapped Loops on page 20). Once this loop is formed, 3 wire ends remain—trim, then fasten them off onto the sides of the wrapped loop with a tight loop. Add a toggle clasp to finish the bracelet.

Pearl & Dangle Earrings

Light-catching square wire forms this elegant pair of earrings that are simpler to make than they appear. One wire forms the main part of the earring, then a dangle is added. The pearls dress up the look of the earrings while a hammered dangle adds movement.

Finished Size: approx. 2" (5.1cm) long × ⁵⁄₈" (1.6cm) wide

materials list

15" (38.1cm) of 22 gauge square wire

4¹⁄₂" (11.4cm) of 22 gauge round wire

2 round pearl 6mm beads

2 jump rings—³⁄₁₆" (5mm), 18 gauge (see pages 23–24 to make your own)

Ear wires (see page 25 to make your own)

Painter's tape

¹⁄₄" (6mm) dowel

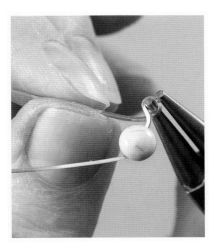

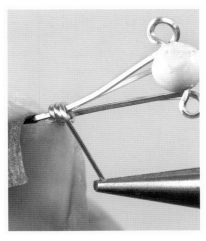

1 Cut 7½" (19cm) of 22 gauge square wire. String a pearl bead onto the wire and center it. Holding the bead in place, bend the wire ends upward. Grasp the wire on the right side of the bead with round nose pliers; bend the wire end downward and around the pliers to form a complete circle. Repeat on the other side of the bead, bending in the opposite direction.

2 Use a pair of chain nose pliers to straighten the loops so they face outward from the bead. Bring the wire ends together. Grasp the wires with round nose pliers 1" (2.5cm) above the bead. Bring the wire ends forward over the pliers to form the top loop of the earring.

3 Bring the wires together beneath the loop, pinching with your fingers. Place a small piece of tape onto the loop to hold the wires together. Cut a 1¼" (3.2cm) length of 22 gauge round wire. Use it to wrap below the loop, fastening the back wires together with the front wires (see Wrapping on page 17). Remove the tape.

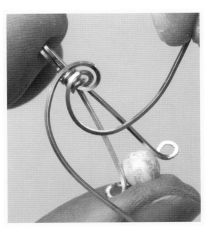

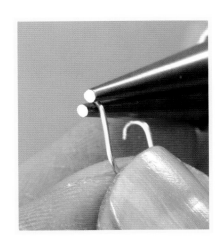

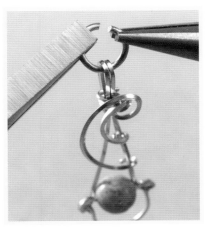

4 Shaping the wire by hand, bring a loose wire end upward and around to form a swirl. Repeat with the other wire end. Trim the ends as needed and fasten each with a tight loop onto the side of the earring (see Tight Loops on page 21).

5 Cut 1" (2.5cm) of 22 gauge round wire and bend it into a U shape over a ¼" (6mm) dowel. Lightly hammer the curved section, then form a loop in each end (see Hammering on page 18). Fasten the loops onto the bottom loops of the earring.

6 Link a 3/16" (5mm) jump ring to the top loop of the earring and fasten it to an ear wire. Make the second earring in the same manner, but reverse the direction of the swirls created in Step 4.

Romance of Jasper Necklace

Deep red beads and wrapped wire are combined in this romantic necklace. Strands of fancy jasper may include rose, deep red, deep green and brown beads. For this piece, I pulled all the deep red beads from the strand to create the look I wanted. This project is for an experienced wire worker.

Finished Size: approx. 16" (40.6cm) long

materials list

61½" (156.2cm) of 20 gauge round wire

99¼" (252.1cm) of 22 gauge round wire

9 faceted pebble fancy jasper 8mm–10mm beads

6" (15.2cm) strand of 4mm round fancy jasper beads

S Clasp (see page 27 to make your own)

Beading wire

4 crimp beads

Painter's tape

Permanent marker

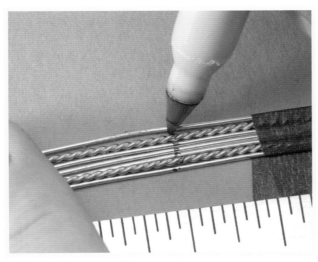

1   Cut a 54" (137.2cm) length of 22 gauge round wire and place both ends side by side in a bench vise. Twist the doubled wire until it is well twisted or until the wires break (see Twisted Wire on page 31). Cut 2 lengths of twisted wire and 5 lengths of 20 gauge wire, each 12" (30.5cm) long. Create a wire bundle with 3 round wires in the middle, a twisted wire at each side of these wires and a round wire at each outer edge. Secure the wire bundle near the center with painter's tape. Mark the wire bundle 6" (15.2cm) from the end with permanent marker.

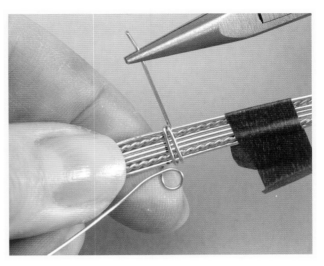

2   Cut 5" (12.7cm) of 22 gauge wire. Wrap the center of the wire around a jaw of a pair of round nose pliers to form a loop. Place the loop below the wire bundle, centered on the mark. Wrap each end of the wire around the bundle 3 times, then trim the ends of the wire (see Wrapping on page 17). On both sides of the loop, shape the wires (keeping them aligned) in a shallow U shape, like the curve of a neckline. As you work, retain this curve.

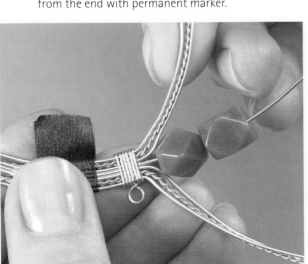

3   Sharply bend 3 wires outward at both the top and bottom of the bundle. String 2 pebble beads onto the center wire.

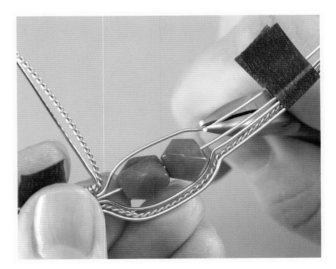

4   Moving the wires 1 at a time, beginning with the innermost wire, shape the lower 3 wires around the beads, keeping the wires in the proper order. Use chain nose pliers to fit them close to the beads. Bend each wire to run parallel to the center wire. Tape these wires. Repeat the shaping with the upper set of wires and tape all of the wires together.

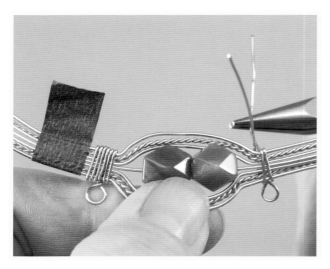

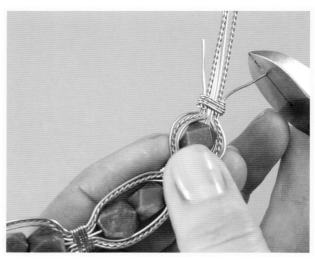

5   Repeat Step 2 after the added beads. Make sure that this and all loops are placed at the lower edge of the piece.

6   Move the 3 upper and 3 lower wires outward again, and string 1 pebble bead onto the center wire. Shape the wires as for Step 4, but keep the outermost wire slightly loose to create a slight gap between it and other wires. Cut a 3½" (8.9cm) length of 22 gauge wire and use it to create a wrap after the single bead.

    Repeat Steps 3–6 to add 2 beads, then 1 bead to the opposite side of the necklace. Trim the outermost upper and lower wires to ⅝" (1.6cm) beyond the wrap.

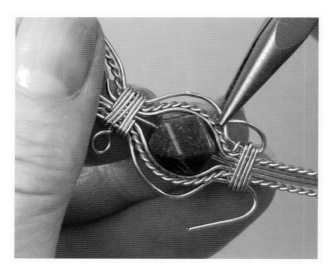

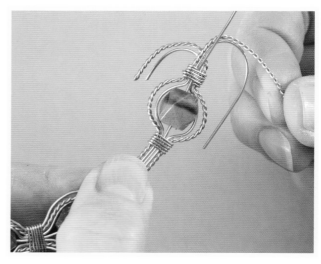

7   Bend the trimmed wires outward and down, and fasten each with a tight loop onto the outermost wire surrounding the single bead (see Tight Loops on page 21).

8   Align the remaining 5 wires and make a mark ¾" (1.9cm) away from the center of the last wrap made. Using 3" (7.6cm) of 22 gauge wire, create a wrap centered on this mark. Move the wires on each side of the center wire outward and string 1 pebble bead onto the center wire. Form the wires around the bead as for Step 4. Using 3" (7.6cm) of 22 gauge wire, make a wrap after the bead. Swirl the outer wires downward.

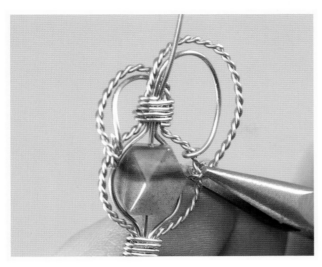

9 Trim the swirled wires as needed and fasten each wire with a tight loop onto the outermost wire surrounding the last bead.

10 Trim the center wire to ½" (1.3cm) and use it to form a plain loop (see Plain Loops on page 19). Finish the opposite side of the necklace in the same manner.

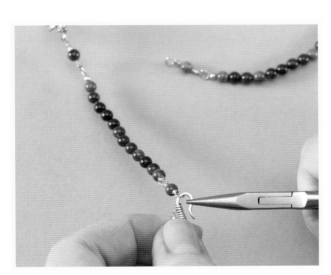

11 Make 4 wrapped bead links—use 2¼" (5.7cm) of 22 gauge wire and a 4mm bead for each (see Bead Links on page 21). Make 2 strands of 4mm beads, each 2" (5.1cm) long, with a wrapped bead link at each end (see Bead Strands on page 30). Fasten a bead strand to each end of the necklace centerpiece. Close the necklace with an S clasp.

12 Make a pebble bead drop with 1½" (3.8cm) of 20 gauge wire and a pebble bead; form a plain loop at one end, string on a pebble bead and form a small curl under the bead (see Bead Drops on page 22). Fasten this drop onto the center loop of the lower edge of the necklace.

Make 2 round bead drops using 1⅛" (2.9cm) of 22 gauge wire and a 4mm round bead for each. Form a plain loop at one end, string on a 4mm bead, then form a small curl under the bead. Fasten a round bead link onto each of the side loops on the lower edge of the necklace.

Pearled Rose Pin

This pin starts with a continuous wire frame, then the petals are filled in with wire bundles that are wrapped, shaped and curled. The pearls, chosen for their uneven, random shapes and mix of colors, are the finishing touch.

Finished Size: approx. 2³/₄" (7cm) wide

materials list

72" (182.9cm) of 22 gauge square wire

21" (53.3cm) of 18 gauge round wire

25" (63.5cm) of 22 gauge round wire

24" (61cm) of 28 gauge round wire

9–12 C and D grade pearl beads in assorted colors, 5mm–6mm in size

1¹/₄" (3.2cm) pin back (see page 29 to make your own)

Painter's tape

Permanent marker

Wire twisting device

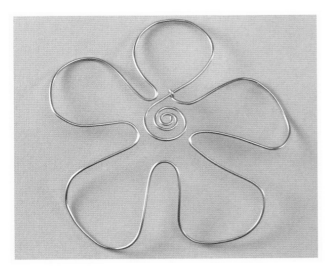

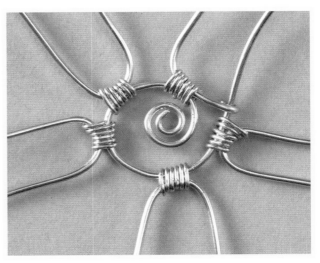

1 To make the rose frame, begin by using round nose pliers to form a small loop in one end of a 21" (53.3cm) length of 18 gauge wire. Change to a pair of flat nose pliers and make an open, flat coil by coiling 3 times around the center loop. By hand, and using pliers as needed, follow the template on page 71 to shape the wire to form 5 petals. Trim the wire as needed and fasten the end with a tight loop around the beginning of the first petal (see Tight Loops on page 21).

2 Cut 5 lengths of 22 gauge round wire, each 2" (5.1cm) long. Use these lengths of wire to wrap the base of each petal to the outer round of the open coil (see Wrapping on page 17).

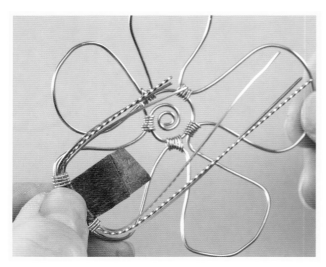

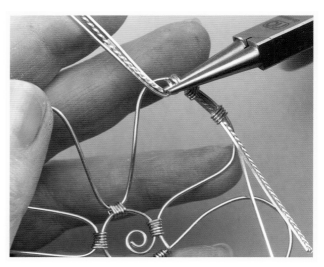

3 Cut 27" (68.6cm) of 22 gauge square wire. Use a wire twisting device to twist the wire until it breaks off (see Twisted Wire on page 31). Cut 2 lengths of untwisted square wire and 1 length of twisted square wire, each 4¹/₂" (11.4cm) long. Bundle the wires with the twisted wire in the middle. Measure and mark 2" (5.1cm) from the end of the bundle. Center a ¹/₂" (1.3cm) wide piece of painter's tape on the mark. Shape the taped area to fit inside the outer edge of one of the petals. Cut 2 lengths of 22 gauge round wire, each 1¹/₂" (3.8cm) long; using these lengths of wire, create a wrap at each side of the tape to connect the wire bundle to the frame.

4 Remove the tape from the wire bundle. Using round nose pliers, grasp the longer end of the wire bundle directly next to the wrap. Form a coil with 2 complete rounds using the tips of the pliers.

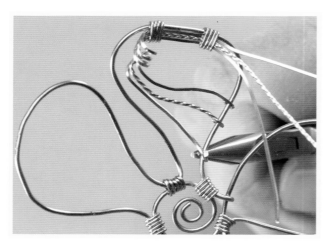

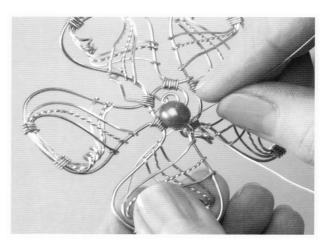

5 Shaping the wires individually into graceful curves, fasten each of the wires from the wire bundle onto the opposite side of the petal. Trim the wires as needed and fasten each with a tight loop onto the frame. Fasten off the shorter ends of the bundle onto the opposite side of the petal. Repeat Steps 3–5 to fill in each petal.

6 Join a 24" (61cm) length of 28 gauge wire to any part of the open coil at the center of the frame with several wraps. Bring the wire to the front, string on a pearl bead, then wrap the wire again onto the open coil.

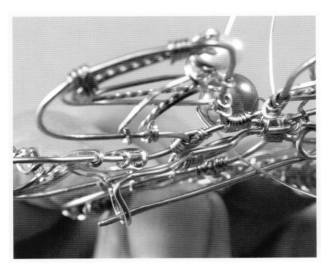

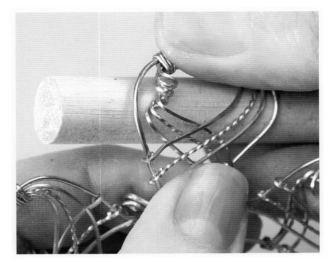

7 Continue to add more pearls to the center of the pin by sewing them on with the 28 gauge wire, and at the same time sew the pin back to the back of the piece with the same length of wire. Attach the pin back on the upper edge of the open coil, not centered on the coil (if the pin back is centered, the pin will droop when worn).

8 Once the center of the pin is filled with pearls and the pin back is secured, end off the 28 gauge wire with a few wraps. To finish the pin, gently bend the petals forward slightly, then round each petal backward a bit over a mandrel or dowel.

template

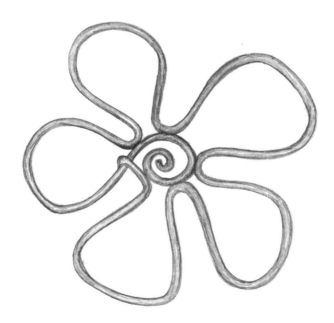

Crystalline Pendant

This elegant piece uses wire and crystal beads to form both a pendant and a bail. Slide it onto a dowel-knitted rope as I have (see the Lariat Necklace on page 136), or use it on a strand of beads or pearls. This is a project for the experienced wire worker.

Finished Size: approx. 1½" (3.8cm) long × ¾" (1.9cm) wide

materials list

18" (45.7cm) of 20 gauge round wire	3¼" (8.3cm) of 22 gauge round wire	1 smooth round crystal 6mm bead
18" (45.7cm) of 22 gauge square wire	27 round glass or crystal 4mm beads in Crystal	1 jump ring—³⁄₈" (1cm), 16 gauge (see pages 23–24 to make your own)
32" (81.3cm) of 24 gauge round wire	1 smooth round crystal 10mm bead	Painter's tape

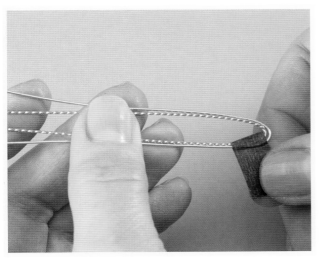

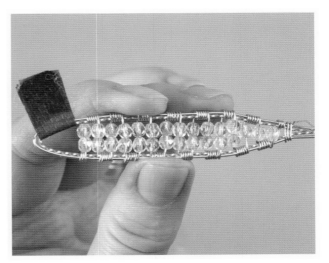

1 Cut 18" (45.7cm) of 22 gauge square wire. Use a wire twisting device to twist the wire until it breaks off (see Twisted Wire on page 31). (If you prefer, you can twist together 2 lengths of 22 gauge round wire instead of 1 length of 22 gauge square wire.)

Cut 1 length of twisted square wire and 1 length of 20 gauge round wire, each 18" (45.7cm) long. Holding them together, grasp the wires at the center with a pair of round nose pliers and bend both ends downward. Place them together with the twisted wire on the inside of the round wire. Place a piece of painter's tape at the bend to hold the wires together.

2 Cut 30" (76.2cm) of 24 gauge wire and fasten it onto the side of the wire bundle created in Step 1 by wrapping it 3 times ½" (1.3cm) below the bend (see Wrapping on page 17). String 2 round crystal beads onto the wire, then wrap the wire at the opposite side of the bend 6 times. Continue in this manner, stringing 2 beads at a time and making 6 wraps at the opposite side, until there are 12 rows of beads.

Bring the wires closer together and string just 1 bead on the wire. Wrap the wire 6 times on the opposite side, add 1 bead and wrap 6 times, add 1 more bead and wrap 3 times. Bring the wires together beneath the last bead. Wrap 3 times around all 4 wires and trim off any excess wrapping wire.

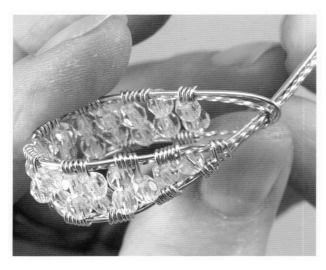

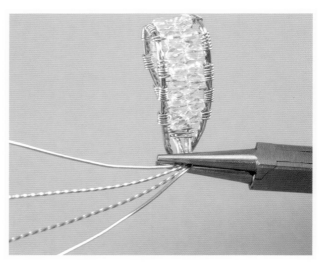

3 Bring the ends of the wire bundle through the ½" (1.3cm) gap above the beads. Carefully curl the piece so the beaded section is rounded approximately at its center. Bend until the final wrap is close to, but not coming through, the ½" (1.3cm) gap.

4 Turn the piece so that the wire ends are to the front. Grasp the wires with a pair of round nose pliers just after the final wrap. One at a time, bring the wires up and toward the left.

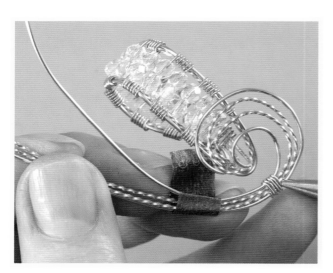

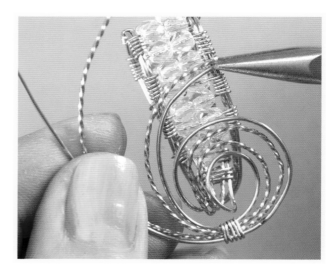

5 Keeping the round nose pliers in place to keep the wires aligned, swirl the wires up and toward the right to form a complete circle. Bring the wires together side by side directly below the point where they emerge from the ½" (1.3cm) gap and tape them together. Cut 2" (5.1cm) of 24 gauge wire and wrap the wires together beneath the swirl.

6 Trimming each as needed, fasten the wires onto the right-hand side of the beaded section with tight loops; fasten the wires into the gaps between wraps (see Tight Loops on page 21).

7 On the back of the piece, use chain nose pliers to angle the wire at the gap backward.

8 Cut 3¼" (8.3cm) of 22 gauge wire. Make a wrapped loop at the end of the wire (see Wrapped Loops on page 20). String a 6mm bead, then a 10mm bead onto the wire. Hammer the wire end, then curl it over the 10mm bead and fasten with a tight loop between the beads (see Hammering on page 18). Attach a ³/₈" (1cm) jump ring to the top of the drop.

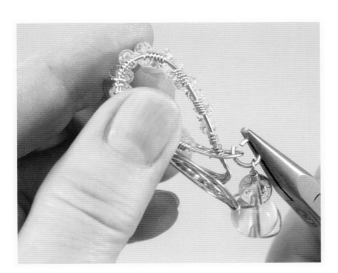

9 Attach the jump ring on the bead drop to the loop on the back of the pendant.

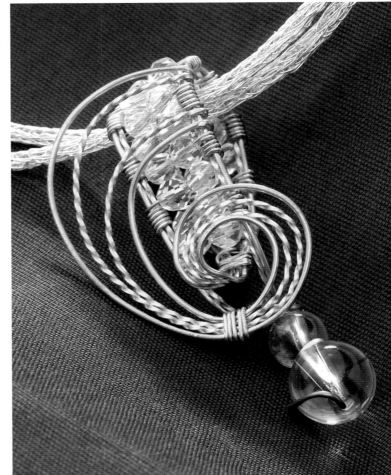

Entwined

A trio of wires entwines a lovely bead to create this ring. Choose a bead that will not break because the bead cannot be replaced once the ring is complete. This is a project for an experienced wire worker.

Finished Size: band is approx. ⁵/₈" (1.6cm) wide; ring diameter variable

materials list

18" (45.7cm) of 20 gauge round wire

18" (45.7cm) of 22 gauge square wire

6" (15.2cm) of 22 gauge round wire

Metal bead approx. 12mm × 12mm with a hole large enough for a pair of 20 gauge wires to pass through

Ring mandrel

Permanent marker

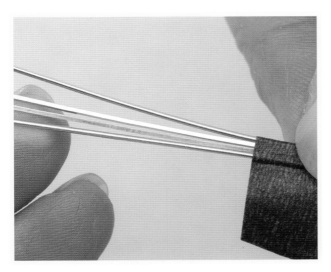

1 Cut 2 lengths of 20 gauge round wire and 2 lengths of 22 gauge square wire, each 9" (22.9cm) long. Bundle the wires together with the square wires between the round wires. Tape the wires together at the center of the bundle.

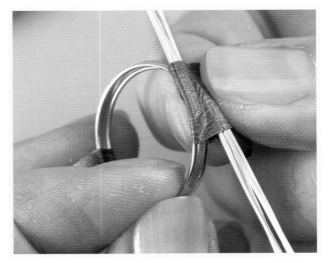

2 Wrap the wire bundle around a ring mandrel at the mark for the ring size you desire. Without mixing the wires from each end of the bundle, tape at the overlap to hold the wires at the correct size.

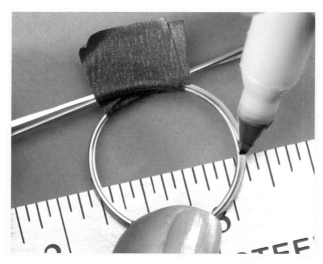

3 Use a permanent marker to mark the sides of the ring at the center; placing the ring on the edge of a metal ruler should help you find the center.

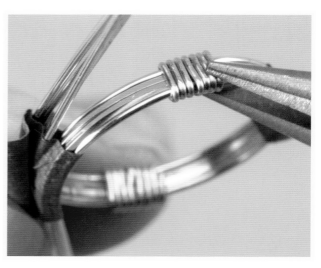

4 Cut 2 lengths of 22 gauge wire, each 3" (7.6cm) long. Wrap these wires over each mark, centering the wraps on the marks and wrapping each wire 6 times (see Wrapping on page 17).

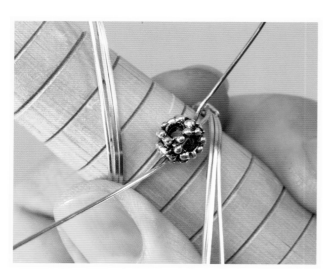

5 Remove both pieces of tape from the wire bundle. Move the 3 outer wires on each side of the ring outward slightly. Place the 2 inner wires through the bead in opposite directions, using chain or flat nose pliers to pull the wires through the bead if needed. Place the ring on the mandrel.

6 Center the bead between the wraps made in Step 4. Bring the ends of the bead wires upward at the sides of the bead. Trim the ends of these wires to 1/2" (1.3cm) beyond the bead.

7 Remove the ring from the mandrel. Hammer the ½" (1.3cm) ends to flatten them slightly (see Hammering on page 18). Use a pair of round nose pliers to curl the ends decoratively at each side of the bead to hold the bead in place.

8 Place the ring on the ring mandrel to be sure the ring size is still the same; as you complete the following steps, occasionally recheck the ring size and make adjustments to the size as needed. Remove the ring from the mandrel and shape the 3 wires on the left side of the bead to swirl over the bead, keeping them aligned. Bring the wires over, then under the band on the right side of the ring.

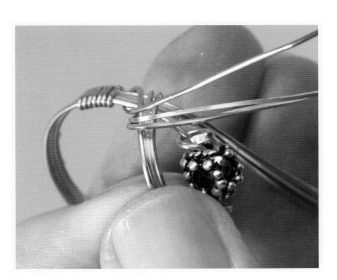

9 Bring the same wire ends forward around the band again.

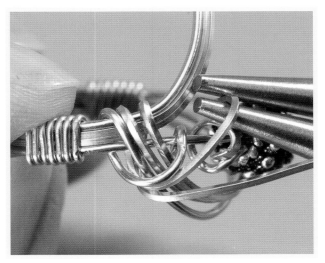

10 Beginning with the wire farthest from the bead, trim and fasten the wires with tight loops individually onto the wire that goes through the bead (see Tight Loops on page 21). Repeat Steps 8–10 to finish the other side of the ring.

wire filigree

The technique we will explore in this chapter, wire filigree, consists of making a flat wire frame that is decoratively filled with shaped wire pieces. The wires within the frame are held to each other and to the frame by wire wraps. The internal decorative wires can be shaped simply or more intricately with specialized hammering and dimensional coils. If you are new to filigree, try the first two projects in this chapter—they are beginner level. The next three projects are for after you've tried your hand at filigree.

Paua Shell Neckpiece

This project combines a hammered wire neckpiece, a jump ring chain, bead drops and an S clasp, plus a joined pair of wire filigree pieces. All of this makes this neckpiece a perfect mix of components for a beginner to have in her repertoire of techniques! If you like, substitute a bead strand to take the place of the jump ring chain.

Finished Size: fits like a 19" (48.3cm) necklace

materials list

10" (25.4cm) of 18 gauge round wire

18" (45.7cm) of 22 gauge round wire

11" (27.9cm) of 16 gauge round wire

4 round amethyst 4mm beads

3 leaf-shaped paua shell 9mm × 15mm beads, drilled at the top

2 jump rings—$^3/_8$" (1cm), 16 gauge (see pages 23–24 to make your own)

92 jump rings—$^3/_{16}$" (5mm), 18 gauge (see pages 23–24 to make your own)

S Clasp (see page 27 to make your own)

Permanent marker

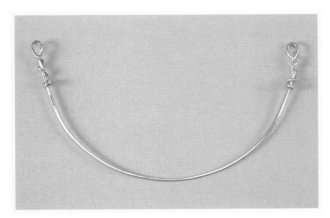

1 Using a pair of round nose pliers, grasp an 11" (27.9cm) length of 16 gauge wire 1$^1/_2$" (3.8cm) from the end. Bend the wire around the jaw of the pliers into a U shape; repeat at the other end. Curve the wire to fit your neck. Hammer the entire wire to flatten it, except for the ends (see Hammering on page 18). Curl the 1$^1/_2$" (3.8cm) ends decoratively, ending with a tight loop around the hammered wire (see Tight Loops on page 21).

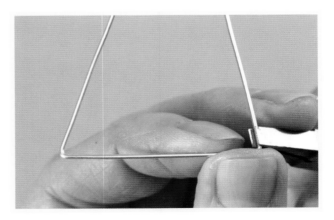

2 Cut 6" (15.2cm) of 18 gauge wire. Use a permanent marker to make marks 2$^1/_8$" (5.4cm) from each end. Using a pair of flat or chain nose pliers, bend each end sharply at the marks.

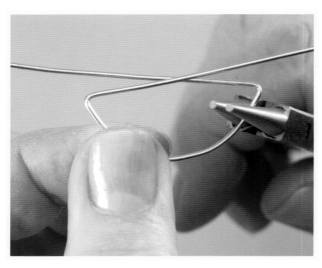

3 By hand, or using round nose pliers if needed, curve the section between the marks to form the rounded bottom of the piece. Bend until the marks are 1¹⁄₈" (2.9cm) apart. The wire ends will cross.

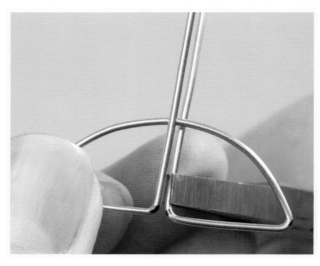

4 Make a mark on each wire where they cross, then use flat or chain nose pliers to bend each end sharply inward at the mark until the wire ends lie side by side.

5 Use a pair of round nose pliers to bend one of the wire ends into a small loop turning away from the center. Switch to chain nose pliers and continue to turn the wire to form an open, flat coil. Repeat with the other end. Check that the coils are side by side and mirror each other.

6 Cut a 4" (10.2cm) length of 18 gauge wire. Make marks 1¹⁄₂" (3.8cm) from each end. Bend each end to a 90 degree angle at the marks. Using round nose pliers, turn one wire end into a small loop turning toward the center of the piece, then switch to chain nose pliers and continue to form an open flat coil. Repeat with the other end. The coils should meet at the center.

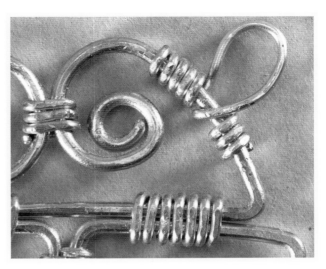

7 Tape the 2 filigree pieces together with their straight edges aligned. Cut 2 lengths of 22 gauge wire, each 2" (5.1cm) long. Use these wires to wrap the 2 filigree pieces together (see Wrapping on page 17). Cut 2 lengths of 22 gauge wire, each 1½" (3.8cm) long. Use these wires to wrap the top coils together and wrap the bottom coils together.

8 Cut 2 lengths of 22 gauge wire, each 3" (7.6cm) long. Using these lengths of wire, make a loop and wrap on each upper curved section of the filigree piece. Follow Steps 1-3 of the Toggle Clasp on page 28 for guidance. Fasten a ³/₁₆" (5mm) jump ring through each loop and around the neckpiece formed in Step 1.

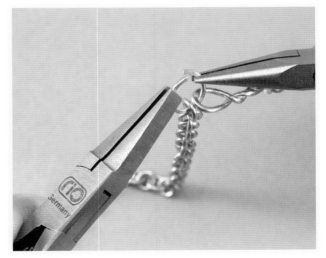

9 Cut 1⅝" (4.1cm) of 22 gauge wire and make a wrapped loop at the end, fastening the length of wire onto the bottom of the filigree piece (see Wrapped Loops on page 20). String on 2 round 4mm beads. Form a small plain loop, then open it slightly and add a paua shell bead to the loop (see Plain Loops on page 19). Use the same method to attach 2 more bead drops, 1 on each side of the first drop. For these drops, use 1½" (3.8cm) of 22 gauge wire and 1 bead each.

10 Assemble the remaining ³/₁₆" (5mm) jump rings into a 10" (25.4cm) chain. Fasten a ³/₈" (1cm) jump ring to each end of the chain. Attach one end of the chain to the neckpiece. Add an S clasp to the other end of the necklace.

Eyelet Links Bracelet & Earrings

The structure of this bracelet is a simple type of link called an eyelet link. Here, the links are rounded and decoratively filled with shaped and beaded inserts. Use the wire of your choice—I chose copper for its reddish, earthy tones. This is an excellent project for a beginner, and a great piece for practicing your wrapping skills!

Finished Size: Bracelet, approx. 7" (17.8cm) long; Earrings, 1³/₄" (4.4cm) long × 1" (2.5cm) wide

materials list

BRACELET

24" (61cm) of 16 gauge round wire

44" (111.8cm) of 18 gauge round wire

76" (193cm) of 22 gauge round wire

8 round malachite 4mm beads

1 jump ring—³/₈" (1cm), 16 gauge (see pages 23–24 to make your own)

Hook clasp (see page 26 to make your own)

Ring mandrel

Painter's tape

EARRINGS

6" (15.2cm) of 16 gauge round wire

11" (27.9cm) of 18 gauge round wire

19" (48.3cm) of 22 gauge round wire

2 round malachite 4mm beads

2 jump rings—³/₈" (1cm), 16 gauge (see pages 23–24 to make your own)

Ear wires (see page 25 to make your own)

Ring mandrel

Painter's tape

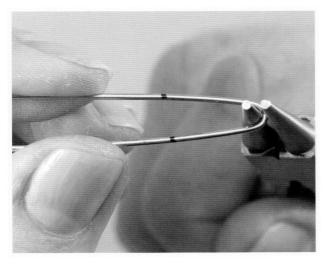

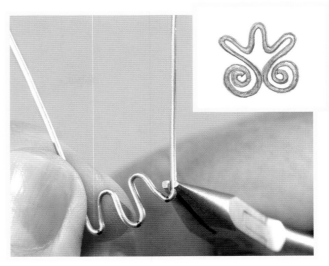

1 Cut 5¹/₂" (14cm) of 18 gauge wire. With a permanent marker, make 3 marks: 1 at the center of the wire (2³/₄" [7cm] from the end) and 1 to each side of the center mark, 2¹/₈" (5.4cm) from each end. Use a pair of round nose pliers to grasp the wire at the center mark and bend the wire to form a U shape.

2 Refer to the template above for the next 2 steps and make sure the wire shape matches the template. Halfway between the center mark and the mark to the left of it, bend the wire sharply downward using chain nose pliers, then bend the wire upward at the mark to the left of the center. Repeat on the other side of the center mark.

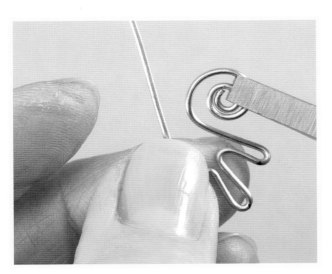

3 Use a pair of round nose pliers to bend one of the wire ends into a small loop turning back toward the center of the wire. Change to chain nose pliers and continue to turn the wire to form an open, flat coil. Repeat on the other end of the wire.

4 Hammer the wire to flatten it (see Hammering on page 18). Shape 7 more lengths of wire in the same fashion.

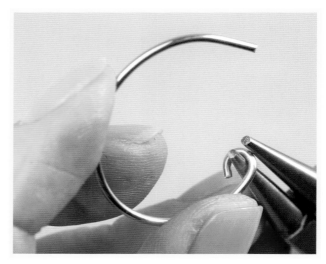

5   Cut a 3" (7.6cm) length of 16 gauge wire. Shape it around the largest part of a ring mandrel so that the ends meet. (When you release the wire, it will spring open a little.)

6   With a pair of round nose pliers, bend each end of the wire into a loop. The loop should be sized so that it will fit slightly loose around a length of 16 gauge wire. Hammer the entire length of wire except for the looped ends. The wire will spread out from hammering.

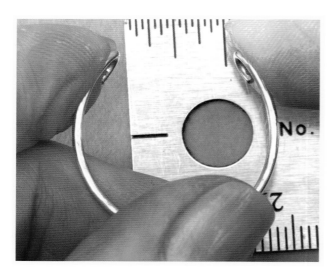

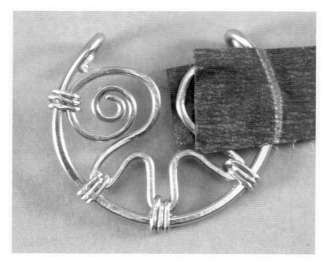

7   By hand, bring the ends together until the gap between them measures 1/2" (1.3cm). Shape 7 more wires in the same fashion.

8   Tape an 18 gauge insert inside a 16 gauge link. Cut 5 lengths of 22 gauge wire, each 1 1/4" (3.2cm) long. Use these wires to make 5 wraps, securing the insert to the frame (see Wrapping on page 17). Trim the wraps as needed so they finish on the back of the piece. Repeat with all inserts and links.

9 Fasten 2 links together by opening out the end loops of one and fastening onto another. Assemble all 8 links in this manner.

10 Cut a 1¼" (3.2cm) length of 22 gauge wire. String a bead onto the wire and center it. Bring the ends downward and insert a wire end through each coil on a wire insert. Wrap the bead onto the insert, fastening the two coils together. Cut 2 lengths of 22 gauge wire, each 1" (2.5cm) long. Make 2 additional wraps on the beaded insert to join the coils to the wires beside them. Add beads and wraps to the other inserts.

11 Finish the unconnected loop end of the final link by bringing the loops close together; join them with a ³⁄₈" (1cm) jump ring. Fasten a hook clasp onto the other end. Working over a dowel or mandrel, carefully round each of the links of the bracelet slightly.

Eyelet Link Earrings

To make matching earrings, follow Steps 1–8 to make 2 individual links. Follow Step 10 to bead each link and add additional wraps. To finish an earring, bring the loops of 1 link close together; join them with a ³⁄₈" (1cm) jump ring. Fasten an ear wire onto the jump ring. Repeat with the other link. Do not round the earring links.

Dragonfly Necklace

A delicate-looking dragonfly is the centerpiece of this necklace; it is enhanced with an amethyst and pearl strand. Unlike the rounded shapes used in the previous filigree projects, this piece features angular bends. Try substituting sharp angles in any project to create a different look. Try this project after you've had a bit of practice in wire working.

Finished Size: approx. 16" (40.6cm) long; dragonfly alone is approx. 2$\frac{1}{2}$" (6.4cm) long × 3$\frac{5}{8}$" (9.2cm) wide

materials list

27" (68.6cm) of 20 gauge round wire

12" (30.5cm) of 22 gauge square wire

43" (109.2cm) of 24 gauge round wire

10mm × 15mm cloisonné bead

10" (25.4cm) strand of amethyst 9mm × 5mm square tube beads

3" (7.6cm) strand of mother of pearl 2mm round beads

2 jump rings—$\frac{3}{8}$" (1cm), 16 gauge (see pages 23–24 to make your own)

2 jump rings—$\frac{3}{16}$" (5mm), 18 gauge (see pages 23–24 to make your own)

S Clasp (see page 27 to make your own)

Beading wire

2 crimp beads

Painter's tape

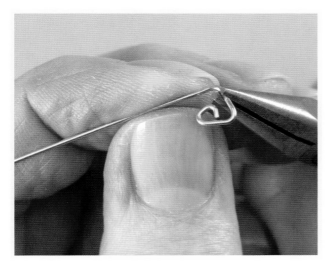

1 Cut 2 lengths of 20 gauge wire, each 3¹/₂" (8.9cm) long. Form one end of each wire by making 4 sharp bends all in the same direction. Use the tips of a pair of chain nose pliers and make the bends as small as possible.

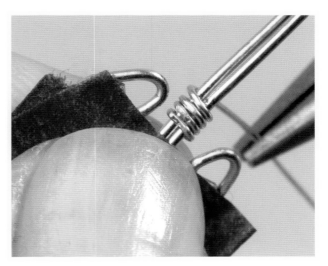

2 Place the 2 wires side by side with the coils facing opposite directions. Tape the wires together at the top of the coils. Cut 18" (45.7cm) of 24 gauge wire. Wrap the end of the 24 gauge wire around the 2 wires several times just beneath the coils (see Wrapping on page 17).

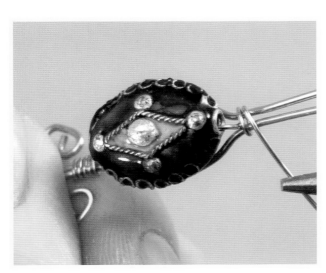

3 Bend the 20 gauge wires outward and bring the 24 gauge wrapping wire between them. String the cloisonné bead onto the 24 gauge wire. Form the 20 gauge wires so they are behind the bead and rounded slightly outward. Bring them together beneath the bead and resume wrapping with the 24 gauge wire.

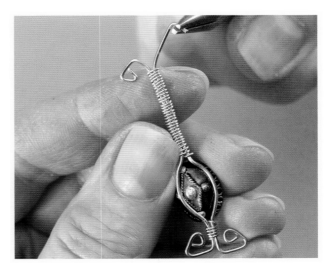

4 Continue to wrap up to within ¹/₂" (1.3cm) of the end of the 20 gauge wires, then end off the 24 gauge wrapping wire. Make 3 small, sharp outward bends in each 20 gauge wire using chain nose pliers. Hammer the coils at each end of the body piece (see Hammering on page 18).

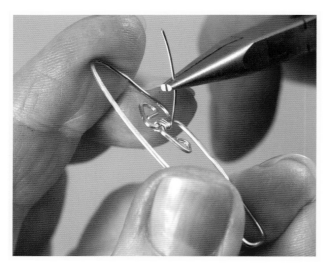

5 Cut a 5" (12.7cm) length of 20 gauge wire. Form one end by making 4 sharp bends all in the same direction. Follow the template at the right to shape the rest of the length of wire. End the wire with 4 sharp bends. Hammer the wire to set the shaping and to flatten it. Use 1½" (3.8cm) of 24 gauge wire to wrap the wires where they meet.

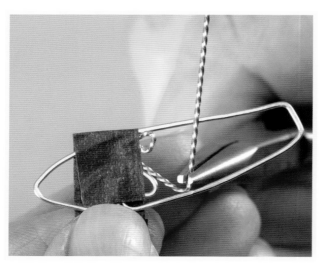

6 Cut 12" (30.5cm) of 22 gauge square wire. Use a wire twisting device to twist the wire until it breaks off (see Twisted Wire on page 31). Cut a 2" (5.1cm) length of the twisted square wire. Bend one end in 3 small, sharp bends. Tape the twisted wire into the hammered wing piece. Make 2 bends to fit the hammered wire into the wing.

7 Shape the end of the twisted wire by making 3 small, sharp bends. Use 1" (2.5cm) lengths of 24 gauge wire to wrap the twisted wire to the wing frame where the wires touch. Make 4 wraps per wing piece. Repeat Steps 5–7 to make a total of 4 wings.

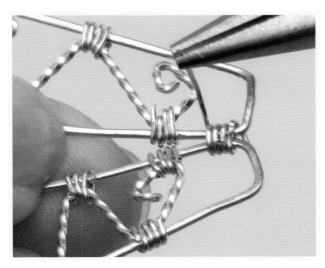

8 Align 2 wings side by side. Use a 1½" (3.8cm) length of 24 gauge wire to wrap the wings together near the base. Repeat to make a second pair of wings.

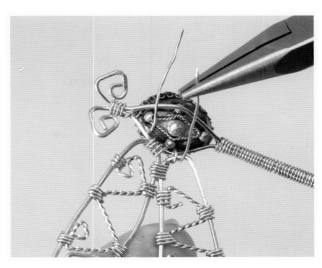

9 Using 3" (7.6cm) of 24 gauge wire for each wing, wrap each pair of wings to the rounded wire behind the bead.

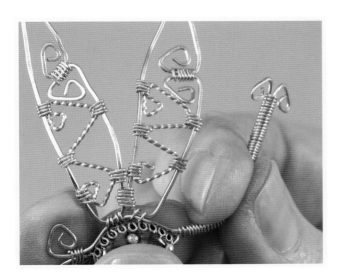

10 Form the wings into gentle curves and curve the body of the dragonfly.

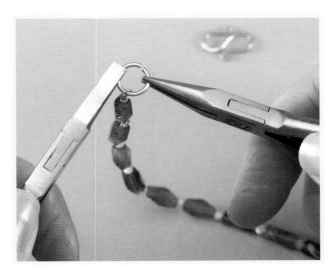

11 Make 4 wrapped bead links—use 2¼" (5.7cm) of 22 gauge wire and 1 amethyst square tube bead for each (see Bead Links on page 21). Make 2 bead strands of alternating amethyst and mother of pearl beads, each 6" (15.2cm) long with a wrapped bead link at each end (see Bead Strands on page 30). Fasten a bead strand to each upper wing of the dragonfly using ³/₁₆" (5mm) jump rings. Fasten a ³/₈" (1cm) jump ring to the free end of each bead strand. Close the necklace with an S clasp.

Rainbow Marble Ring

Marble is a beautiful stone, but it is soft. Use it for jewelry that won't be worn every day, or in settings in which the stone is well protected. The instructions for this wide-band ring are size specific. If you wish to change the dimensions for your own ring, you will need to redesign the interior pieces to fit a smaller or larger frame. To do this, use inexpensive practice wire and keep track of how much wire is needed so you can translate your changes into a finished piece. This is a good intermediate project if you make it in the size given; resizing the ring will take more skill.

Finished Size: band is approx. ³/₄" (1.9cm) wide at the bead portion; instructions are for a size 9 ring

materials list

18" (45.7cm) of 18 gauge round wire

10" (25.4cm) of 20 gauge round wire

27¹/₂" (69.9cm) of 24 gauge round wire

14mm coin-shaped rainbow marble bead

Painter's tape

Ring mandrel

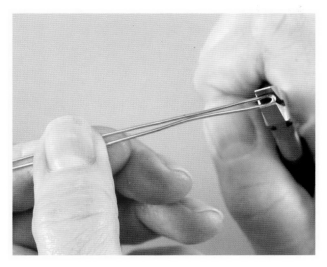

1 Grasp the center of an 18" (45.7cm) length of 18 gauge wire with round nose pliers and bend it in half. Compress the bend using a pair of flat nose pliers to bring the two wire ends side by side.

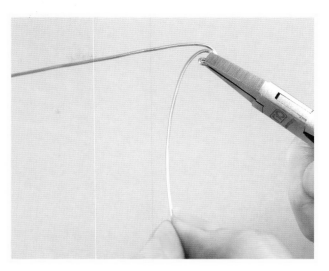

2 Grasp the bend in the wire using flat nose pliers and, one at a time, bring the ends around by hand to form a doubled-wire flat spiral. Use the template below as a reference when shaping the wire.

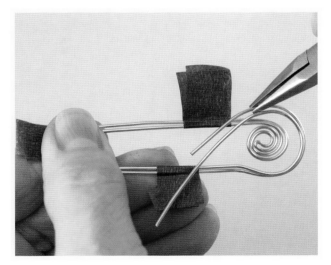

3 Keeping the wires side by side throughout, follow the template at right to shape the frame. Use round, chain or flat nose pliers as needed to form the piece. Use tape as needed to hold the form until the ends are finished off.

template

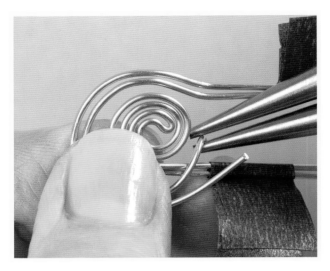

4 Fasten off each wire end onto the frame with a tight loop (see Tight Loops on page 21). Hammer the frame lightly except for the tight loops (see Hammering on page 18).

5 Cut 2 lengths of 20 gauge wire, each 5" (12.7cm) long. Form each wire separately by following the template below. Hammer each wire lightly.

6 Fit the inserts side by side within the frame, reshaping as necessary, and tape them in place. Use 1¹/₂" (3.8cm) lengths of 24 gauge wire to wrap the inserts to the frame (see Wrapping on page 17). Wrap every place that the interior pieces touch the frame, and where the interior pieces touch. Remove the pieces of tape as you proceed with the wraps.

template

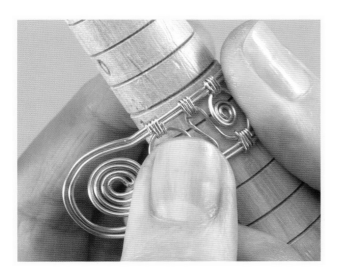

7 Wrap the ring around a ring mandrel to shape it. Because the shank is wide, turn the ring around on the mandrel to shape the opposite side of the ring. Take the ring off the mandrel and tweak as needed with pliers to form it into a perfect round.

8 Cut a 2" (5.1cm) length of 24 gauge wire and use it to create a wrap connecting both ends of the frame.

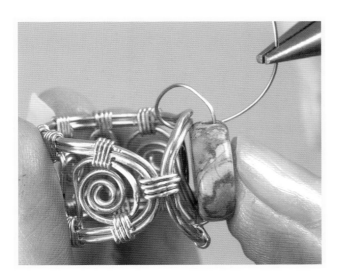

9 Fasten the bead above the frame's coil using 6" (15.2cm) of 24 gauge wire: Wrap one end of the 24 gauge wire 3 times around the bottom of the coil, then string the bead onto the wire and wrap the wire 3 times on the top of the coil. Cross the wire behind these wraps and wrap 3 times at the other side of the bead wire. Run the wire back through the bead and finish off with 3 more wraps. (This makes 6 wraps on each side of the bead.)

Filigree Elements Necklace

Three filigree elements provide focal points within this glass pearl necklace. Make the elements, then string them into the necklace as if they were beads. The internal coils are made of hammered wire with a variation on the flat coil that creates a tighter and finer-looking coil. This project is for intermediate level wire workers.

Finished Size: approx. 16" (40.6cm) long including clasp

materials list

33" (83.8cm) of 18 gauge round wire

120" (304.8cm) of 24 gauge round wire

19½" (49.5cm) of 20 gauge round wire

100 round metal 2.5mm beads

16" (40.6cm) strand of teal glass pearl 6mm beads

6 metal spacer 5mm × 3mm beads

S Clasp (see page 27 to make your own)

Beading wire

2 crimp beads

Permanent marker

Painter's tape

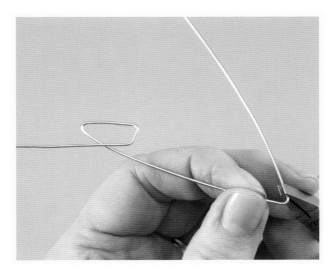

1 Cut 11" (27.9cm) of 18 gauge wire. Working from one end, use a permanent marker to place marks at 5" (12.7cm), 8" (20.3cm), 8¾" (22.2cm) and 9" (22.9cm). Use flat or chain nose pliers to make a sharp bend at each mark; make every bend in the same direction.

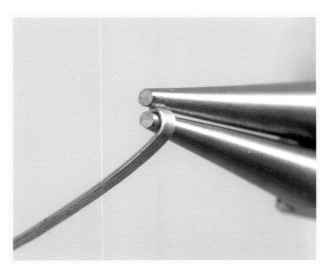

2 Turn the wire sideways (do not lay it flat) and hammer 1" (2.5cm) of the shorter end and 2" (5.1cm) of the longer end (see Hammering on page 18). Using round nose pliers, grasp the shorter flattened end and roll it into a tight, closed coil, leaving a small hole at the center for the beading wire.

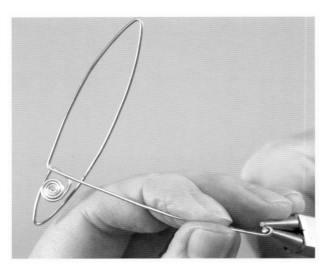

3 Bend the longer end to fit directly against the coil. Form the longer end into a ¹/₂" (1.3cm) wide closed coil; make the final round of the coil open. Lightly hammer the outer edges of the frame.

4 Use 2" (5.1cm) of 24 gauge wire to wrap the 2 coils together (see Wrapping on page 17).

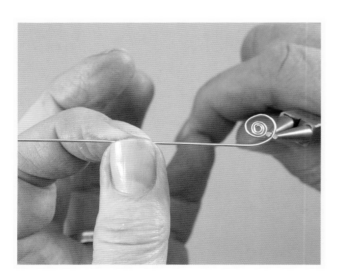

5 Cut a 6¹/₂" (16.5cm) length of 20 gauge wire. Hammer 1¹/₂" (3.8cm) of one end and make a tightly closed coil; make the final round of the coil open. Repeat on the last 2" (5.1cm) of the wire, forming the coil in the opposite direction.

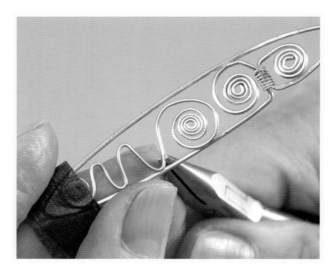

6 Tape the smaller coil into the frame near the bottom end. Bend the wire into a W shape to fit within the frame; the loops of wire should touch the frame. Arrange the upper coil so that it touches the larger coil in the frame and meets both side edges of the frame. Take the shaped wire out of the frame and hammer it lightly between the coils, then tape it back into the frame.

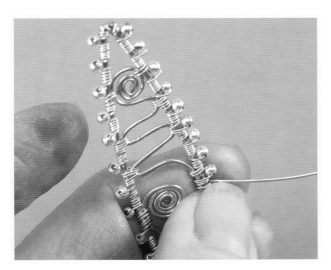

7 Cut 36" (91.4cm) of 24 gauge wire. Fasten this wire with a few wraps onto the outer edge of the frame, anywhere on the frame. Continue to wrap the wire around the frame, working over parts of the interior wire as you come to them, and adding a 2.5mm bead onto the wire every 6 wraps. Using a 2" (5.1cm) length of 24 gauge wire, wrap the larger coil of the interior piece to the larger coil of the frame.

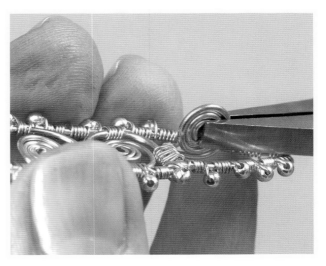

8 Turn the smaller coil of the frame to the back of the piece. Repeat Steps 1–8 to make 2 more identical filigree elements.

9 Make 2 wrapped bead links—use 2¼" (5.7cm) of 22 gauge wire and 1 pearl bead for each (see Bead Links on page 21). Make a bead strand with a wrapped bead link at each end (see Bead Strands on page 30). String 2 pearl beads, 1 spacer bead, 21 pearl beads, 1 spacer bead, 3 pearl beads, a filigree element, 2 pearl beads, 1 spacer bead, 2 pearl beads, a filigree element (this is the necklace center), then finish the strand mirroring the first half. Close the necklace with an S clasp.

CHAPTER FIVE

wire crochet

Crochet has much to offer the jewelry artist. A single layer of crocheted fine wire offers an open, airy look that is delicate and feminine while strands of crocheted chain have an ethereal look. Crocheted wire can be stretched against clear plastic tubing to create a shadowy texture much like wool crepe fabric. For a denser piece, crocheted wire can be stacked in layers. Beads can enhance any of these looks—slide beads onto the wire beforehand and crochet them into the piece, sew them on after a piece is complete, or encase them between layers. To learn how to crochet (and don't be timid—it's one of the easiest fabric-creating skills out there) turn to pages 104–105.

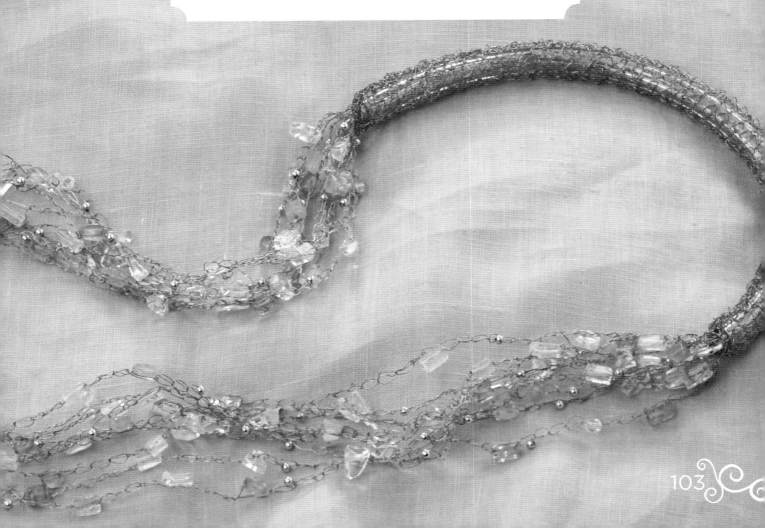

Wire Crochet Techniques

If you have never crocheted before, do not try to learn using wire. Start by using worsted weight yarn and a U.S. size G/6 (4mm) crochet hook. Once you feel comfortable with those items, change to crochet thread and a small steel crochet hook to practice making finer stitches. When you are confident with that combination, then try crocheting with practice wire.

Wire Gauges for Crochet

I like to work with wire in gauges 30, 32 and 34 for wire crochet. I find 32 gauge wire to be ideal for most projects, but I turn to 30 gauge wire if I want a fabric that is a little firmer. Wire that is heavier than 30 gauge is more difficult to crochet with. A 34 gauge wire creates a more gossamer-like stitch than 32 gauge wire, and it may be tricky for beginners because it is a very fine wire. I recommend a size 7 steel crochet hook with any of these wire gauges.

If you are familiar with knitting or crochet, you may be aware of a kind of gauge other than wire gauge. In knitting and crochet, gauge refers to the number of stitches per inch of the finished fabric. Gauge is important in crocheting garments, but it is not needed for the jewelry projects here. Most pieces here are made to a certain length or width or to fit within a frame, so you do not need to try to match your crochet gauge to mine as you work.

Crochet Stitches

There are many different kinds of stitches you can make in crochet. Crochet stitches used in this chapter are given here as a reference. As you work, shape each stitch as it is made to fit just a bit loosely on the hook as shown at the right. If stitches are made too tightly, it will be difficult to work into them in later rows or rounds. If the stitches are too loose, the "fabric" will look sloppy and the resulting piece will also be larger.

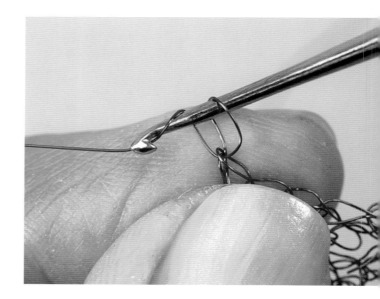

Slip Knot

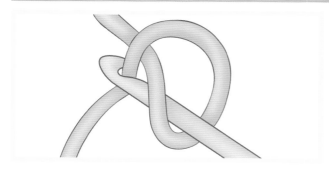

1 Create a loop near the end of the wire. Insert the hook into the loop and catch the wire connected to the spool of wire.

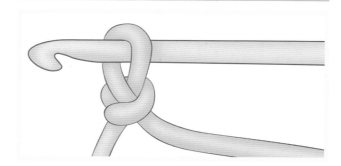

2 Pull the wire on the hook through the loop. Tighten the knot until it is close to the hook.

Chain Stitch (ch)

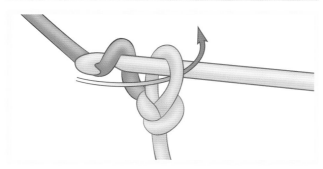

1 Wrap the wire around the hook, and draw it through the loop on the hook. This creates a new loop on the hook. Repeat for the desired length of chain.

Slip Stitch (sl st)

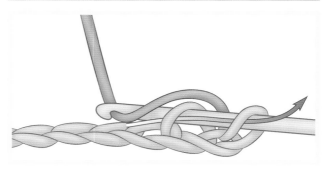

1 Insert the hook into a stitch, wrap the wire around the hook, and draw the wire through both loops on the hook.

Single Crochet (sc)

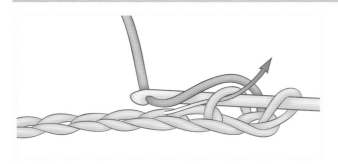

1 Insert the hook into a stitch, wrap the wire around the hook, and draw the wire through only the first loop on the hook. There are now two loops on the hook.

2 Wrap the wire around the hook again and draw the wire through both loops on the hook.

If your instructions call for a stitch increase (inc), work two stitches into a single stitch; this will increase your stitch count in a row or round by one. If your instructions call for a stitch decrease (dec), skip a stitch in the row or round you are working; this will decrease your stitch count in a row or round by one. To end a piece of crochet, cut the wire and bring the end through the final loop. Pull the final loop snug.

Beaded Crochet

Working beads into crochet is easy to do. Begin by stringing beads onto the wire you'll be using for a project. It's best to string more beads than you think you'll need in case of miscounting. Beads can be added into chain stitches and single crochet stitches. As you crochet, the beads will end up on the back of the piece. If you are crocheting a flat piece, beads can be added every other row. If you are crocheting in the round, beads can be added to every round.

To add a bead into a single crochet stitch, insert the hook into the next stitch. Slide a bead up the wire to the crochet hook. Finish the stitch as described above.

To add beads into a crochet chain, draw up the loop on the hook to the same height as the bead, slide the bead up to hook and finish the stitch as described above.

Pearled Tube Bracelet

This bracelet begins with a single crochet piece worked flat, then shaped around plastic tubing. Finishing the bracelet is as simple as wrapping the tube with pearls and adding a clasp. Make several of these so you can wear two or three at a time, or so you can give them as gifts.

Finished Size: 8" (20.3cm) long including clasp

materials list

10 yds. (9.1m) of 32 gauge round wire

24" (61cm) of 22 gauge round wire

9" (22.9cm) of 16 gauge round wire

8" (20.3cm) strand of round glass pearl 4mm beads

6³/₄" (17.1cm) of clear plastic tubing with a ¹/₄" (6mm) outside diameter (look for this at a hardware store)

S Clasp (see page 27 to make your own)

Size 7 steel crochet hook

Sewing needle with eye large enough to fit 32 gauge wire

Painter's tape

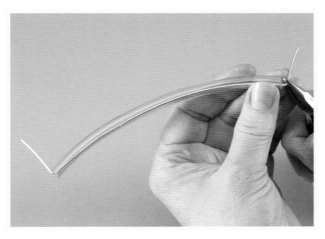

1 Run a 9" (22.9cm) length of 16 gauge wire through a 6³/₄" (17.1cm) length of plastic tubing. Center the tube on the wire. Using a pair of chain nose pliers, sharply bend each end of the wire to secure the tube onto the wire.

2 To make the crocheted piece, using a size 7 steel crochet hook and 32 gauge wire, make a crochet chain 1" (2.5cm) long (see Chain Stitch on page 105). Work flat in single crochet for 6¹/₄" (15.9cm) (see Single Crochet on page 105).

Cut the wire being crocheted, leaving an end about 18" (45.7cm) long. Thread the end of the wire through the eye of a sewing needle. Stitch the crocheted piece around the plastic tube, gathering the piece tightly around the 16 gauge wire at each end. Finish off the 32 gauge wire ends by weaving them into the crochet using a sewing needle, then trim the wire ends close to the surface.

3 String 8" (20.3cm) of pearl beads on a 24" (61cm) length of 22 gauge wire. Center the beads on the wire and place a piece of tape at each end of the beads to keep them in place. Coil the beaded section around the crochet covered tubing, making the coils evenly spaced about ¹/₈"–¹/₄" (3mm–6mm) apart. Center the coiled beads on the tubing, then remove the piece of tape from one end. Wrap the wire end tightly and evenly around the tube. Repeat at the other end.

4 Use round nose pliers to form a loop at the end of the 16 gauge wire, then curl the remaining wire back and forth decoratively. Hammer the ends flat (see Hammering on page 18). Close the bracelet with an S clasp.

Floating Crystals Necklace

Single crochet stitches and chain stitches form this delicate looking, airy, light-catching necklace. The clear crystal beads almost seem to float on the chained strands while the light amethyst ones add subtle hints of color. Worked in the round with plastic tubing to add shaping, this piece is easy to wear—slip it on and the curved back will hug your neck and stay in place.

Finished Size: approx. 32" (81.3cm) long

materials list

34 yds. (31.1m) of 30 gauge round wire

12" (30.5cm) of 16 gauge round wire

12" (30.5cm) strand light amethyst 7mm × 4mm square tube beads

12" (30.5cm) strand crystal quartz 7mm × 4mm square tube beads

12" (30.5cm) strand crystal quartz chip beads

48 round metal 2.5mm beads

9" (22.9cm) of clear plastic tubing with a ¼" (6mm) outside diameter (look for this at a hardware store)

Size 7 steel crochet hook

Sewing needle with eye large enough to fit 30 gauge wire

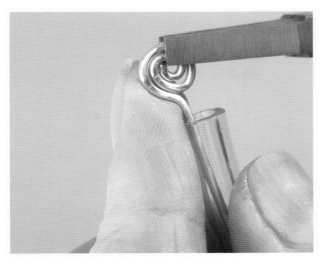

1 Run a 12" (30.5cm) length of 16 gauge wire through 9" (22.9cm) of plastic tubing. Center the tube so that equal amounts of wire protrude at each end. Form each end into a closed flat coil.

2 Remove the beads from their strands, place them into a bowl and mix them. Randomly string 36" (91.4cm) of beads onto 30 gauge wire; keep the wire uncut, and work off the spool for this step and the following steps. Using a size 7 crochet hook and 30 gauge wire, make a crochet chain 9" (22.9cm) long (see Chain Stitch on page 105). This will be the back of the necklace. Continue to make chain stitches for an additional 23" (58.4cm) of chain while randomly incorporating 16–20 beads (see Beaded Crochet on page 105). Lightly stretch this length after crocheting it.

To begin the second round, work in single crochet, adding no beads, across the beginning 9" (22.9cm) of chain (see Single Crochet on page 105). Once you have worked across the unbeaded 9" (22.9cm) portion of chain, chain for 23" (58.4cm) as before, randomly adding beads. Continue to work around until there are 9 complete rounds (9 beaded strands and 9 rows of single crochet) or until the single crochet section measures 1" (2.5cm).

3 Cut the wire being crocheted, leaving an end about 24" (61cm) long. Thread a sewing needle onto the end of the wire. Place the single crochet portion of the necklace over the plastic tube. Sew the long edges of the crocheted piece together. Sew each end closed around the wire above the coil. Finish off the 30 gauge wire ends by weaving them into the crochet using the sewing needle, then trim them closely. Form the back of the necklace into a U shape to fit your neck.

Trio of Crocheted Earrings

This trio of earrings uses crocheted wire to create different effects. In the easy-to-make Captured Bead Earring, a bead is enclosed within two layers of single crochet. For the best effect, choose a translucent or light-catching bead. The Dagger Earring also features a double layer of crochet, but this time the crocheted wire is formed within a wire frame. For best results, pay close attention to the shaping of the frame—it is slightly curved, not straight. With a little care, these are fairly easy to make. The last earring, the Coral Donut Earring, uses crochet worked in the round. This earring has interesting cupolini beads around the outer edge and is finished with a bead in the center. This pair is for experienced crocheters.

Finished Size: Captured Bead Earrings, crocheted portion approx. 1" (2.5cm) square; Dagger Earrings, approx. 2" (5.1cm) long without ear wire; Coral Donut Earrings, crocheted portion approx. 1¹⁄₄" (3.2cm) in diameter

materials list

FOR ALL
Ear wires (see page 25 to make your own)

Size 7 steel crochet hook

Sewing needle with eye large enough to fit 32 gauge wire

CAPTURED BEAD EARRINGS
7 yds. (6.4m) of 32 gauge round wire

8" (20.3cm) of 20 gauge round wire

2 round fluorite 8mm beads

DAGGER EARRINGS
7 yds. (6.4m) of 32 gauge round wire

12" (30.5cm) of 20 gauge round wire

2 round ocean jasper 6mm beads

CORAL DONUT EARRINGS
14 yds. (12.8m) of 32 gauge round wire

6" (15.2cm) of 20 gauge round wire

96 red coral cupolini 5mm–15mm beads

2 round flower jasper 6mm beads

Captured Bead Earrings

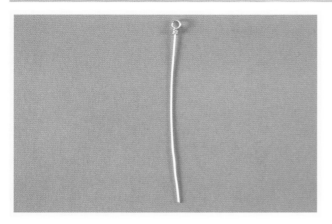

1 Cut 4" (10.2cm) of 20 gauge wire and make a wrapped loop at one end (see Wrapped Loops on page 20).

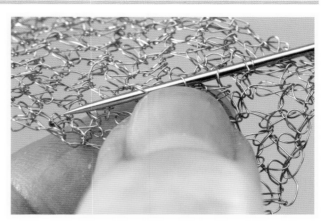

2 Using 32 gauge wire and a size 7 crochet hook, chain 9 stitches (see Chain Stitch on page 105). Turn the work, chain 1, and work in single crochet over the original 9 chain stitches; the piece should measure 1" (2.5cm) wide (see Single Crochet on page 105). *Turn, chain 1, and work across the row in single crochet; repeat from * until the piece measures 2" (5.1cm) long. Fasten off, leaving an end about 12" (30.5cm) long for sewing. Weave the starting end of wire into the crocheted mesh.

3 Fold the crocheted piece in half to make a 1" (2.5cm) square. Insert the 20 gauge wire piece made in Step 1 into the middle of the folded edge. Thread a sewing needle onto the end of the wire left for sewing. Sew the layers together along one edge, working toward the folded edge at the top of the piece. Sew across the folded edge, working around the base of the wrapped loop. Continue to sew around the edge until you get to the 20 gauge wire coming through at the bottom of the square. Sew halfway across the bottom edge, then string an 8mm bead onto the 20 gauge wire. Move the bead so that it is within the crocheted square. Finish sewing the square closed. Do not end off the wire.

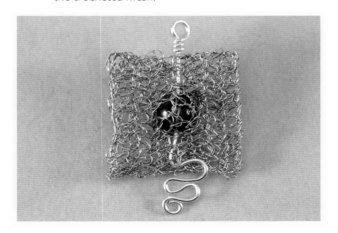

4 Center the bead inside the square. Run the needle through stitches up to the bead, then stitch through both layers around the bead. Finish off the 32 gauge wire end by weaving it into the crochet using the sewing needle, then trim the end close to the surface. Using a pair of chain nose pliers, bend the 20 gauge wire end sharply to one side, then shape the wire into a zigzag or a spiral. Fasten an ear wire to the top loop. Make a second earring that mirrors the first.

Dagger Earrings

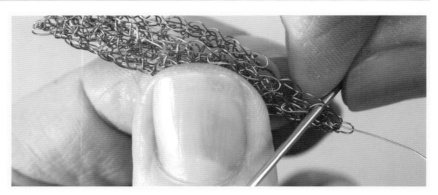

1 Cut a 6" (15.2cm) length of 20 gauge wire. Using a pair of round nose pliers, make a loop in one end (see Plain Loops on page 19). Follow the diagram above to make a total of 3 sharp bends in the wire and shape the long edges into gentle curves.

2 Using a size 7 crochet hook and 32 gauge wire, chain 12 stitches (see Chain Stitch on page 105). Turn the work, chain 1, then work 12 single crochet along the chain (see Single Crochet on page 105). Turn, chain 1, work a single crochet in each of the next 10 stitches (leave 2 stitches unworked). Turn, skip 1 stitch and work a single crochet in each of the remaining 9 stitches. Fasten off the 32 gauge wire.

Make a second piece like the first, leaving 18" (45.7cm) of wire on the second piece for sewing. Finish off all wire ends except the sewing wire by weaving them into the mesh of the crochet.

Thread a sewing needle onto the 18" (45.7cm) wire end. Hold the two crocheted pieces back-to-back, then sew them together around all outer edges. Do not fasten off the sewing wire.

3 Place the sewn piece inside the 20 gauge wire frame and stitch the piece to the frame all around. Compress the mesh as needed to fit it within the frame. Do not fasten off the sewing wire.

4 Take a couple of stitches toward the upper center of the crochet piece. String a 6mm bead onto the wire and sew through the crocheted wire, then come up again to secure the bead to the earring with a second stitch. Finish off the wire ends by weaving them into the crochet using the sewing needle, then trim close to the crochet wire.

Using chain nose pliers, bend the protruding 20 gauge wire end downward beneath the beginning loop and to the side, forming a graceful curve. Bend the wire at the side of the earring, bring it across the back of the earring, then bend the wire to the front below the bead. End the wire by tucking it into the crochet mesh. Push gently on the back of the crochet mesh to mound it outward slightly. Add an ear wire to the top loop. Make a second earring that mirrors the first.

Coral Donut Earrings

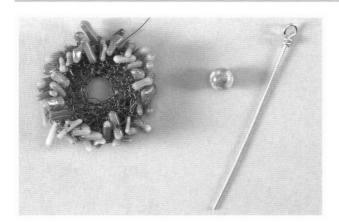

1 Cut 3" (7.6cm) of 20 gauge wire and make a wrapped loop at one end (see Wrapped Loops on page 20). String 48 cupolini beads onto the 32 gauge wire; keep the wire uncut, and work off the spool for this step and the following steps.

Using a size 7 crochet hook and 32 gauge wire, chain 6 stitches (see Chain Stitch on page 105). Work a slip stitch into the first chain stitch to form a ring (see Slip Stitch on page 105). Work the following pattern:

Round 1: Chain 1, then work 12 single crochet into the ring (see Single Crochet on page 105). Join the round with a slip stitch into the beginning chain.

Round 2: Chain 1, work 2 single crochet into each single crochet of the previous round. Join the round with a slip stitch into the beginning chain.

Round 3: Chain 1, work 1 single crochet into each single crochet of the previous round, adding a coral bead into each stitch (see Beaded Crochet on page 105). The beads will settle onto the back side of the work. Join the round with a slip stitch into the beginning chain.

Round 4: Repeat Round 3.

Round 5: Chain 1, work 1 single crochet into each single crochet of the previous round. Join the round with a slip stitch into the beginning chain.

Rounds 6 and 7: Chain 1, work 1 single crochet into every other single crochet of the previous round. Join the round with a slip stitch into the beginning chain.

Fasten off leaving at least 12" (30.5cm) of wire.

2 Run the 20 gauge wrapped loop wire through the crocheted donut, carefully working it through the mesh of the crochet from the top to the bottom, poking holes with a sewing needle if needed. As you work the wire through, add a 6mm bead to the wire at the center of the donut. Push the wire through until the wrapped loop rests against the crocheted mesh. Using chain nose pliers, sharply bend the bottom of the wire toward the back of the earring. Thread a sewing needle onto the end of the 32 gauge wire and sew the final crocheted round to the starting round, working around the center of the donut. Run the needle up to the wrapped loop and make a few stitches to snug the crocheted mesh around the wrapped loop. Finish off the wire ends by weaving them into the crochet using the sewing needle, then trim closely.

3 At the bottom of the earring, form the 20 gauge wire into a closed flat coil. Use chain nose pliers to bend the coil upward against the back of the donut. Fasten an ear wire to the wrapped loop. Make a second earring in the same way.

Beaded Leaf Pin

A combination of graceful lines, colorful beaded crochet and swirls of wire give this pin an air of elegance. Try switching the color of your crochet wire to turn this from a spring-green leaf to an autumnal piece of jewelry. This is an intermediate level project, so I don't recommend it as your first crocheted wire piece.

Finished Size: approx. 2³/₄" (7cm) long

materials list

15" (38.1cm) of 18 gauge round wire

3" (7.6cm) of 24 gauge round wire

1¹/₄" (3.2cm) of 20 gauge round wire

17 yds. (15.5m) of 34 gauge round wire

70 size 11/0 seed beads that match the 34 gauge wire

15mm × 6mm tear-shaped flourite bead

Size 7 steel crochet hook

Sewing needle with eye large enough to fit 34 gauge wire

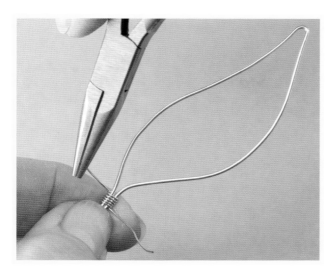

1 Using a pair of flat nose pliers, bend a 15" (38.1cm) length of 18 gauge wire 5" (12.7cm) from the end; this bend will be the tip of the leaf. Shape the leaf by hand, or using pliers if needed, following the template on page 117. Follow the curves as closely as possible because the shape is important to the finished design. Use a 3" (7.6cm) length of 24 gauge wire to wrap the wire ends where they come together.

2 String 70 seed beads onto the 34 gauge wire. If your beads are on a strand, you can tie one end of the strand onto the end of the wire, then run the beads onto the wire. Keep the wire uncut and work off the spool for this step and the following steps.

Using a size 7 crochet hook and 34 gauge wire, chain 18 stitches (see Chain Stitch on page 105). Turn the work, chain 1, then work 18 single crochet stitches along the chain, adding a bead into each stitch (see Single Crochet and Beaded Crochet on page 105). Turn the work, skip the first single crochet, then work a single crochet in each of the next 16 single crochet, adding a bead into each stitch. Repeat this row 3 times, but reduce the number of stitches each time, going from 14 stitches to 12 stitches to 10 stitches. After a total of 5 rows have been worked, fasten off. Check that the size of the crocheted piece is close to the size of the frame. Follow the instructions above to make 2 more crocheted pieces, but do not add beads. Leave a 30" (76.2cm) tail of wire on the third piece. Finish off the ends on each piece by working them into the mesh of the crochet. Thread a sewing needle onto the 30" (76.2cm) wire end. Hold the 3 crocheted pieces together with the beaded piece on top. Sew the pieces together all the way around, catching the edges of each piece in each stitch. Do not cut the sewing wire.

3 Place the piece within the frame made in Step 1. Stitch around, sewing through the edge of the crocheted piece and around the wire of the frame with each stitch. Make the stitches about 1/8" (3mm) apart, and form the crocheted piece to fit inside the frame as you go. Do not cut the wire (the end will be used later to secure the catch).

4 Grasp the shorter 18 gauge wire end with round nose pliers just above the 24 gauge wrap made in Step 1. By hand, or using chain nose pliers if needed, bring the end downward to form a loop around the jaw of the round nose pliers, then go behind the wrap made in Step 1. Bring the end around the wrap to the front and then again to the back of the piece.

5 Use a pair of chain nose pliers to bend the end into a U-shaped catch at the back of the piece. Sew the catch to the fabric of the crocheted wire to secure it in place, then end off the 34 gauge sewing wire by working it back and forth several times through the back of the crochet, and trim it close to the surface.

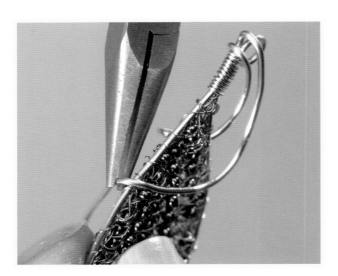

6 Using chain nose pliers, bend the longer 18 gauge wire end sharply downward over the 24 gauge wrap made in Step 1, then curve it gracefully over the top of the pin. Bend the wire to the back of the pin.

7 Bring the wire diagonally across the back of the pin. Shape this part of the wire so it is curved against the back of the crochet, rounding the crochet outward toward the front of the piece. Then, bring the wire across the front of the crochet again near the tip of the leaf shape.

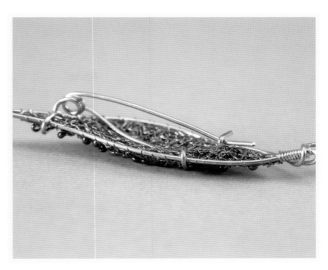

8 Bend the wire again to the back of the work and flatten the wire against the back. The rest of the wire will now be used to form a pin back. To form the coil of the pin back, use chain nose pliers to bring the wire upward in a 90 degree bend. Switch to a pair of round nose pliers and form a double coil on the tips of the pliers.

9 Bring the wire over to the pin catch, and trim it to ¼" (6mm) beyond the catch. Finish the pin end (see Pin Back on page 29).

template

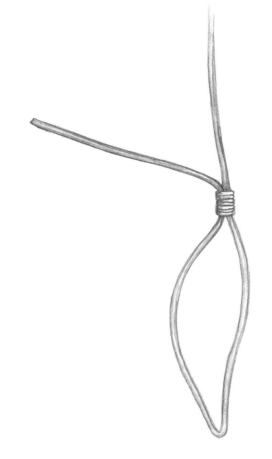

10 Make a bead drop with 1¼" (3.2cm) of 20 gauge wire and a teardrop bead; form a plain loop at one end, string on the teardrop bead and form the other end into a plain loop as well (see Bead Drops on page 22). Fasten the upper loop of the drop to the loop of the pin.

Nested Charms Bracelet

Frilly crochet provides a "nest" for the bead charms in this bracelet. The charms serve a dual purpose: not only are they decorative, but they also fasten the crocheted wire to its base! Adjust the size of the wire frame as needed to achieve a close fit.

Finished Size: approx. 7" (17.8cm) long including clasp

materials list

300 yds. (274.3m) of 32 gauge round wire

13" (33cm) of 16 gauge round wire

1³/₈" (3.5cm) of 20 gauge round wire for each stone bead (use longer wires for decorative drops)

Selection of semiprecious stone beads that will fit onto 20 gauge wire

1 jump ring—³/₈" (1cm), 16 gauge (see pages 23–24 to make your own)

Hook clasp (see page 26 to make your own)

Size 7 crochet hook

Sewing needle with eye large enough to fit 32 gauge wire

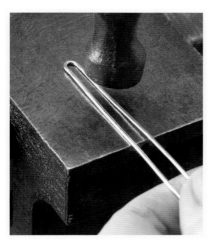

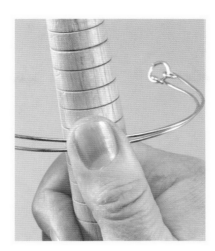

1 Cut 13" (33cm) of 16 gauge wire. Grasp the wire at the center using a pair of round nose pliers; bend the wire until the ends are parallel with a ⅛" (3mm) gap in the middle. Hammer the doubled wire, avoiding the last ½" (1.3cm) of each end (see Hammering on page 18).

2 Use round nose pliers to bend each end of the 16 gauge wire into a small loop. Place a ⅜" (1cm) jump ring onto both of the loops. Curve the piece into a cuff shape, rounding it over a ring mandrel or other rounded form, then fit it to your arm.

3 Create a variety of plain loop drops using 20 gauge wire and assorted semiprecious beads (see Bead Drops on page 22). I recommend making at least 30 charms. Start each drop with a plain loop, add a bead and finish with a decorative loop, coil or swirl.

4 Using a size 7 crochet hook and 32 gauge wire, make a crochet chain 6" (15.2cm) long (see Chain Stitch on page 105). Turn the work and follow this pattern:

Round 1: Chain 1, work a single crochet in the next chain stitch and in each chain stitch to the end of the chain (see Single Crochet on page 105). In the last chain stitch, work 3 single crochet stitches. Do not turn the work, but begin working on the other side of the chain and make a single crochet in each chain stitch through the unused loop on the chain. At the opposite end of the chain, make 3 single crochet stitches into the end loop. Continue to work in continuous rounds for the rest of the piece.

Round 2: Work a single crochet stitch in each single crochet of the previous round, making 3 single crochet stitches in the end stitch at each end.

Round 3: Work 2 single crochet stitches in each single crochet of the previous round.

Round 4: Repeat Round 3.

Round 5: Work a single crochet stitch in each single crochet of the previous round. Finish off the wire ends by weaving them into the crochet using the sewing needle, then trim close to the surface of the fabric.

To assemble the bracelet, use the charms to fasten the crocheted piece onto the wire frame. Hold the crocheted piece against the wire frame and fasten each charm onto one of the 2 wires of the frame through the crocheted mesh by opening out the plain loop, working it through the mesh of the crochet and around the wire frame. Distribute the charms evenly between the 2 wires of the frame, keeping the larger drops toward the center of the piece. Fasten a hook clasp onto the rounded end of the wire frame.

dowel knitted wire

Dowel knitting, which is also sometimes called Viking knitting, is created by hand-forming stitches in a circle around a dowel rod or other cylindrical form. This creates a tubular rope that can be used in all types of jewelry. It is a very old technique—some of the ancient jewelry pieces I saw on display at the Louvre were exquisitely dowel knitted using very fine wire. Those meticulously hand-formed early art pieces were my inspiration for the pieces in this chapter. Dowel knitting may seem like a very basic technique, but it can be used in stunning ways in jewelry designs. Learn the basic steps of dowel knitting on pages 122–127, then experiment by changing the basic variables to create your own jewelry designs.

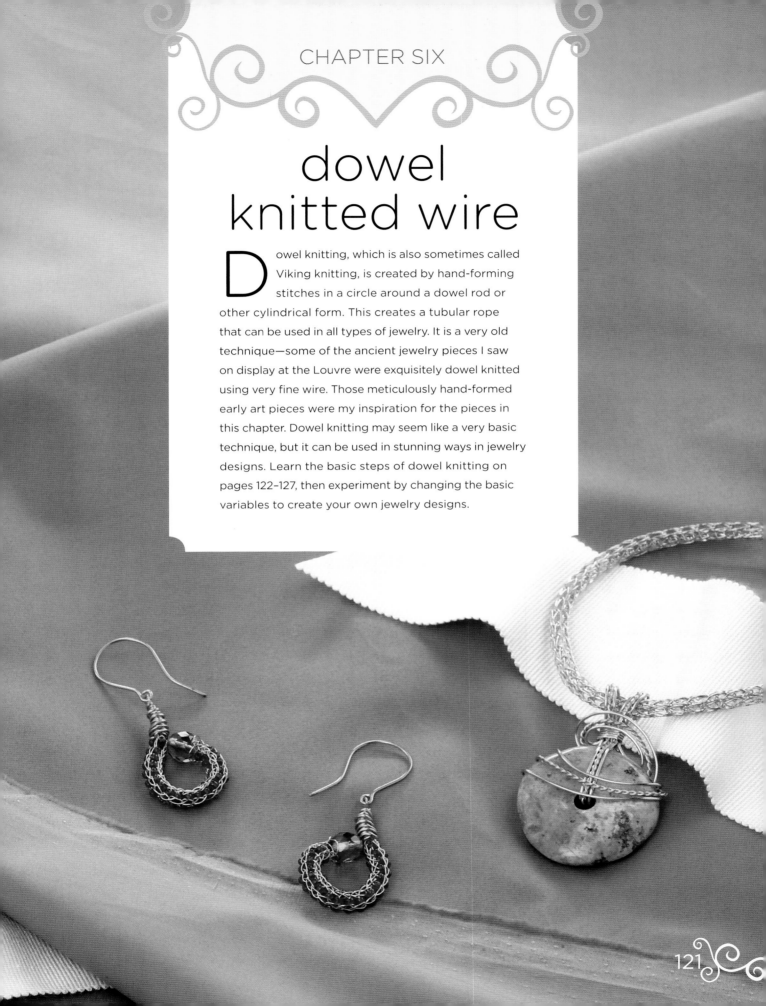

Dowel Knitting Techniques

The process of dowel knitting is different from regular knitting. Follow the instructions over the following pages to learn the basics, then experiment to create your own variations. When you are creating a project, don't get caught short! It's best to knit a longer rope than you think you need. You cannot add to a dowel-knitted rope once it has been drawn through a drawplate, but you can always trim off extra rope if your piece is too long.

Dowel Knitting Tools and Materials

Dowel knitting is a simple process that only requires a few items: a dowel rod or other cylindrical form, a harness and wire. Variations in these three items will give your work different looks.

Dowel Rod

In dowel knitting, you form your knitted tube around a dowel rod or other cylindrical form. To create different looks, you can change the size of the dowel you form your piece around. A dowel with a $3/16$" (5mm) diameter is the smallest size I'd recommend; however, you can go larger if you wish, up to any diameter you are willing to work on.

Harness

The harness is an item you create yourself (see instructions on page 123), and it is used as the foundation of your knitted rope. Most projects will call for a harness with three to six petals. The more petals in a harness, the denser the finished piece will be.

Wire

Wire is used to form the actual wire knitting, so it has the most influence over the finished look of your piece. I find wire gauges 26–32 the most workable for dowel knitting; 26 and 28 gauge wires are the easiest for beginners. Gauges heavier than 26 can be difficult to form into knit stitches, especially as the wire work hardens. Even with 26 gauge wire I sometimes feel the need to use a pair of chain nose pliers to settle a stitch into place. Fine gauge wires such as 32 gauge must be threaded onto a sewing needle for use in dowel knitting because the wire is too soft to maneuver through the stitches. Fine wires also kink easily. If you are working with fine wire, keep the wire as straight as possible, because forcing a kink through a stitch can break the wire.

I recommend using plain, uncoated wire if the dowel-knitted rope will be pulled repeatedly through a drawplate for resizing; coated wires will lose their coating during repeated draws through a drawplate. Save colorful coated wire for projects made of 30 or 32 gauge wire where less force is needed, and then use a drawplate gently.

The amount of wire you'll need for dowel knitting will vary according to wire gauge, number of harness petals, size of dowel, type of knit and size of stitches. To give you some idea of how much wire is used, however, 2 yds. (1.8m) of 26 gauge wire makes about $1 1/2$" (3.8cm) of single dowel-knitted rope (before using a drawplate), if you are using a 6-petal harness on a $1/2$" (1.3cm) dowel; 2 yds. (1.8m) of 28 gauge wire makes approximately 1" (2.5cm) of double dowel-knitted rope using the same setup. The wire amounts given for the larger ropes throughout this chapter are approximate. Stock up on plenty of wire before beginning a project.

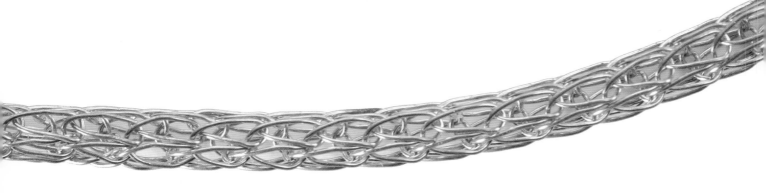

Creating a Harness

All dowel-knitted ropes, whether single or double knit, begin on a harness. This will be scrapped later, so it is made of base metal wire. The first round of stitches will be formed on the loops (petals) of the harness, and later the harness serves as a handle for pulling the knitted rope through the drawplate. After pulling the finished rope through a drawplate, remove the harness either by snipping the loops of the harness or by snipping through the stitches of the first round of knitting. If the harness is removed intact, it may be reused.

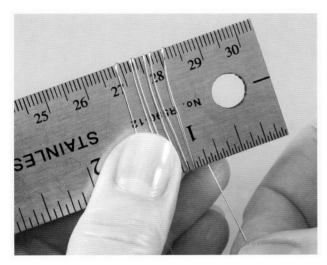

1 To make a harness, gather the following items: a dowel rod, a metal ruler, masking tape and round wire in the base metal of your choice. For these instructions, I am using a 6" (15.2cm) dowel rod that is ¹/₂" (1.3cm) in diameter and 20" (50.8cm) of 26 gauge round wire.

Wrap the end of the base metal wire around the ruler once for each petal in your harness. I am making a 6-petal harness, so I have made 6 complete wraps.

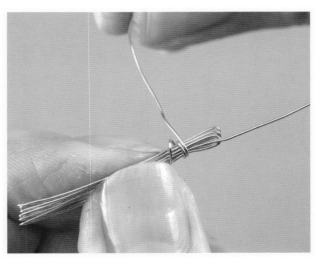

2 Slide the wraps off of the ruler. Using one of the loose ends of the wire, make several wraps around the bundle toward the end.

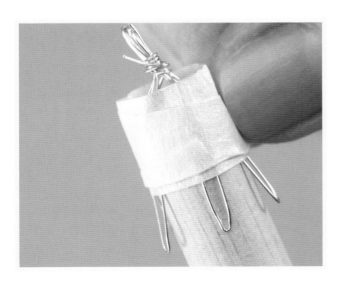

3 Open out the petals of the harness and place the center of the bundle onto the end of the dowel. Fold the petals downward against the dowel. Wrap the upper part of the harness with masking tape to hold it in place. You are now ready to begin dowel knitting.

Single Dowel-Knitted Rope

If you are new to dowel knitting, start with a single dowel-knitted rope. I've chosen 26 gauge wire because it's a good weight for beginners to start with, and yet it makes a great-looking rope for a necklace. The single knit stitch is slightly more open than the denser double knit but is equally attractive after drawing it out using a drawplate.

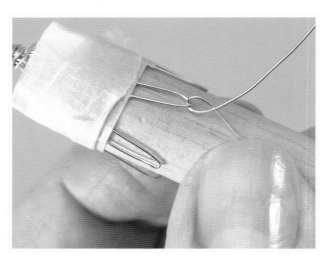

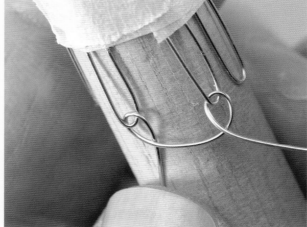

1 Cut a length of 26 gauge wire (or the gauge called for in your project), approximately 1 yd.–2 yds. (91.4cm–182.9cm) long—a shorter length is suitable for beginners; you can use longer lengths of wire as you gain more experience.

Thread approximately 1" (2.5cm) of the wire through a petal on the harness (you can choose any petal on the harness). Thread the wire from the front of the petal to the back. Hold the end against the dowel with your thumb.

Pick up the long end of the wire and cross it over the wire end toward the next petal. The photos here show working from left to right around the dowel. You can work left to right as I did, or you can work from right to left if you prefer. It doesn't matter in which direction you proceed, but work in the same direction for the entire project.

2 Thread the long end of the wire through the next petal from the front to the back with the wire end pointing toward the previous stitch. Do not pass the long end of the wire under any wire except the petal wire. Cross the wire end over itself toward the next petal and pull the wire all the way through the petal until a small loop forms.

3 Place your thumb over the stitch you just made and hold it in place as you make the next stitch. As you form the stitches, keep them evenly spaced. Repeat Step 2 until you've gone all the way around and a stitch has been made in every petal of the harness.

When you are ready to begin the second round of stitches, make the stitches in the same way, but pass the wire end behind each stitch made in the previous round instead of through the harness petal. At times, you may find it necessary to use a large sewing needle to adjust the previous round in order to pass the wire through.

Double Dowel-Knitted Rope

A double dowel-knitted rope is as easy to make as a single dowel-knitted rope. The main difference is that this technique makes a more densely knitted rope, which may be preferable for some projects. Try both single dowel-knitted rope and double dowel-knitted rope to see the difference. Because of the denseness of the weave in a double dowel-knitted rope, I suggest using a finer wire gauge, such as 28 gauge wire.

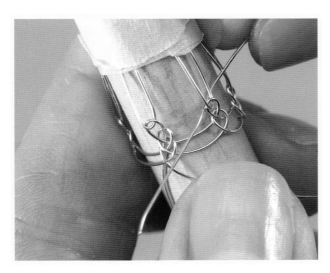

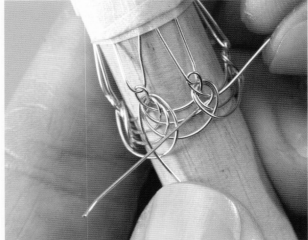

1 Follow the instructions for Single Dowel-Knitted Rope (see page 124) to complete 2 rounds of knitting. Work the third round by passing the wire behind the loops of the first round—you are working over 2 rounds here, instead of 1 as you did for Single Dowel-Knitted Rope.

2 Work the fourth round by passing the wire behind the loops of the second round. Continue to knit by working over 2 rows for each stitch.

Triple Dowel-Knitted Rope is worked in the same manner as double knitted, except stitches are worked over three rows instead of two.

Adding More Wire

Unless you are making a very small piece, you'll need to end a wire and begin a new length at some point. When you are down to your last 1" (2.5cm) of wire, trim the wire end to about ½" (1.3cm). Cut a new length of wire and slide the end under the loop of the final stitch, leaving a new ½" (1.3cm) tail. Begin dowel knitting with the new length of wire. As you come around to the tails, work over them—do not slide the new wire under the tails. The tails will be inside the tube when it is finished. Continue to knit and add wire until the rope is the length needed.

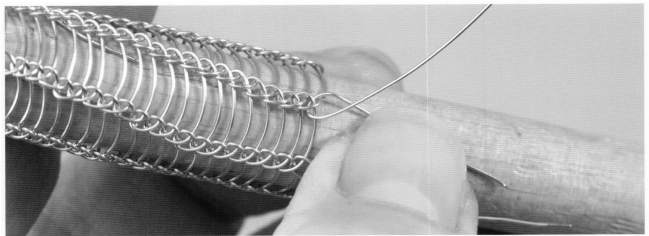

Using a Drawplate

The secret to a beautifully smooth and even-looking rope is to use a drawplate. This process lengthens and compacts your stitches. Your first attempt at dowel knitting may come off the dowel looking rather coarse, but you will be amazed at the difference after using a drawplate. A single dowel-knitted rope may double in length depending on the size of the dowel and the number of petals used, while a double-knitted one may finish to be about one and a half times the original length.

1 To draw the rope through the drawplate, begin with a hole slightly smaller than the rope. Compress the harness with your fingers, push it through the hole and grab onto it with a pair of flat nose pliers.

2 Take a firm hold on the drawplate and pull the rope through in one even motion. Next, pull the rope through the next smaller hole. Continue pulling the rope through consecutively smaller holes until the rope cannot be drawn smaller or until it is the size needed. Remove the harness from the rope.

End Caps and Loops

Finish your dowel-knitted rope with a combination wrapped end cap and loop. This makes a neat finish for the rope and provides loops for a clasp at the same time. The length of wire needed for wrapping the end cap will vary according to the number of wraps made, and the circumference of the dowel-knitted rope. Work this in practice wire before using a more expensive wire.

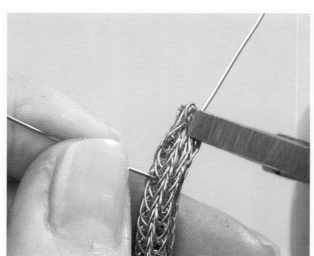

1 Cut a length of wire for the end cap and loop following your project's instructions. Here, I'm using 15" (38.1cm) of 22 gauge round wire. Push the end of the wire into and through the dowel-knitted rope $\frac{1}{2}$" (1.3cm) from the end until $1\frac{1}{2}$" (3.8cm) of wire protrudes from the rope. Using a pair of flat nose pliers, squeeze the end of the rope to taper it against the wire. Next to the rope, bend the long end of the 22 gauge wire into a 90 degree angle.

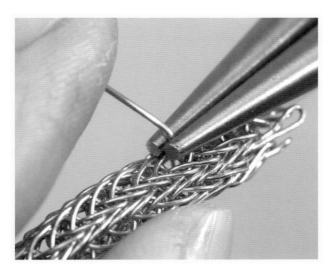

2 Grasp the wire at the base of the bend using round nose pliers. Begin wrapping the wire around the rope. Put aside the pliers as soon as you can get the wrapping going by hand.

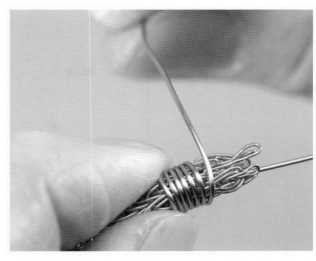

3 Wrap by hand, keeping the wraps even and snug to each other. Wrap up to the end of the rope, then finish with a couple of wraps around the 22 gauge wire. Cut the wrapping wire.

4 Finish the 22 gauge wire by forming a loop on the largest part of the round nose pliers' jaw. This loop can be a wrapped loop or a plain loop (see Wrapped Loops on page 20 and Plain Loops on page 19). Trim the wire end as needed.

Bead-Encrusted Bracelet

Sewing beads onto this dowel-knitted bracelet creates a surface that sparkles with the rich colors of gemstones. Add as many beads as you like to make the bracelet decorative and light-catching. The beads placed before and after each gemstone conceal the sewing wire on either side of the bead and at the same time add sparkling highlights. Add some decorative chains and you will appear to be wearing three bracelets at once!

Finished Length: approx. 7³/₄" (19.7cm) long including clasp

materials list

7 yds. (6.4m) of 28 gauge round wire

30" (76.2m) of 26 gauge round wire

22" (55.9cm) of 20 gauge round wire

20" (50.8cm) of 26 gauge round wire in a base metal of your choice

24 gemstone beads in assorted sizes, shapes and colors (or more if desired)

2.5mm round metal beads, 2 for each gemstone bead

38 jump rings—³/₈" (1cm), 16 gauge (see pages 23–24 to make your own)

38 jump rings—³/₁₆" (5mm), 18 gauge (see pages 23–24 to make your own)

Hook clasp (see page 26 to make your own)

¹/₄" (6mm) dowel rod

Masking tape

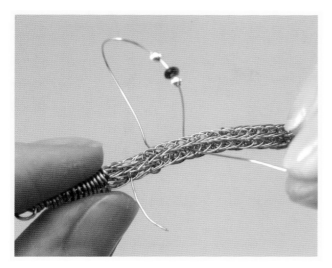

1 Use 20" (50.8cm) of 26 gauge base metal wire to make a 6-petal harness. Tape it to the end of a 1/4" (6mm) dowel rod. Using 28 gauge wire, make a 5" (12.7cm) long double dowel-knitted rope (see Double Dowel-Knitted Rope on page 125). Pull the dowel-knitted piece through a drawplate until it is approximately 3/16" (5mm) in diameter (see Using a Drawplate on page 126). Trim the rope to 6 3/4" (17.1cm). Use 11" (27.9cm) of 20 gauge wire to make an end cap and loop at one end of the rope (see End Caps and Loops on pages 126–127). Repeat at the other end.

Cut a 30" (76.2cm) length of 26 gauge wire. Fasten it onto the end of the dowel-knitted tube by sewing through the tube a few times with the wire. No sewing needle should be needed. Work the end of the wire carefully through the mesh of the dowel knitting to make each stitch. To sew on the beads, string a 2.5mm bead, a gemstone bead, then another 2.5mm bead onto the wire. Sew the wire back through the dowel-knitted tube, pulling the beads snug to the surface of the tube. String another bead sequence onto the wire, and sew it onto the bracelet. Continue to sew on beads in this manner; as you work, place smaller beads farther apart near the ends of the tube, and larger beads close together at the center. Sew the beads on one side of the tube only in order to have no beads at the side of the tube that will be against your arm. End off the sewing wire by making a few stitches through the mesh of the dowel knitting.

2 Make 2 chains, each 7" (17.8cm) long, by alternating 3/8" (1cm) and 3/16" (5mm) jump rings. Fasten the ends of the chains to the end cap loops.

3 Add a 3/8" (1cm) jump ring to each end cap loop. Attach a hook clasp to one of these jump rings.

Captured Pearls Necklace

Enmeshed pearls shine through the knitted wire fabric of this elegant necklace. The single dowel-knitted rope is formed by hand (no drawplate needed) over a core of glass pearls. You can dowel knit the rope using your choice of 28 gauge wire or 30 gauge wire.

Finished size: approx. 16" (40.6cm) long including clasp

materials list

10 yds. (9.1m) of 28 gauge or 30 gauge round wire

30" (76.2cm) of 20 gauge round wire

42³/₄" (108.6cm) of 22 gauge round wire

20" (50.8cm) of 26 gauge round wire in a base metal of your choice

36 round glass pearl 4mm beads

18 round glass pearl 6mm beads

25 round glass pearl 8mm beads

6 round glass pearl 10mm beads

Size .012" (.31mm) beading wire

13 jump rings—³/₈" (1cm), 16 gauge (see pages 23–24 to make your own)

S clasp (see page 27 to make your own)

¹/₂" (1.3cm) dowel rod

Masking tape

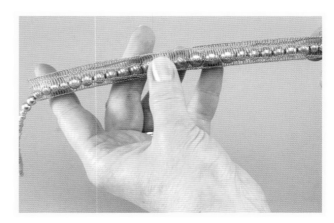

1 String the pearl beads onto the beading wire in this order: 18, 4mm beads; 6, 6mm beads; 6, 8mm beads; 6, 10mm beads; 6, 8mm beads; 6, 6mm beads; 18, 4mm beads. To finish each end of the bead strand, run the beading wire over the end bead and through the next bead. Tie a knot in the wire, then run the wire through the next bead. Repeat this until there are 4 knots, then run the wire through several more beads and trim off the excess wire.

2 Use a 20" (50.8cm) length of 26 gauge base metal wire to make a 6-petal harness. Tape it to the end of a ¹/₂" (1.3cm) dowel rod. Using 28 gauge or 30 gauge wire, make a 7" (17.8cm) long single dowel-knitted rope (see Single Dowel-Knitted Rope on page 124). Remove the tube from the harness but do not compress it. Place the bead strand inside the dowel-knitted tube and center it.

3 Keeping the bead strand centered and starting at the center, carefully run your fingers over the tube and pull it outwards, working a short section at a time. Gradually form the tube to fit snugly over the beads. There will be a small amount of tube extending beyond the bead strand at each end. If needed, trim each end to 1" (2.5cm) past the beads. Use 15" (38.1cm) of 20 gauge wire to make an end cap and loop at one end of the rope (see End Caps and Loops on pages 126–127). Repeat at the other end. Use an S clasp to connect the end loops.

4 Make 13 wrapped bead drops using 2¹/₄" (5.7cm) of 22 gauge wire and a single 8mm bead for each (see Bead Drops on page 22). Form a wrapped loop in one end, string on an 8mm bead, hammer the wire end, then curl it up and over the bead and fasten with a tight loop above the bead (see Hammering on page 18).

Next, make 6 wrapped bead links using 2¹/₄" (5.7cm) of 22 gauge wire and a single 6mm bead for each (see Bead Links on page 21). Fasten each wrapped bead link onto a wrapped bead drop as the second wrapped loop is made on the link.

5 Find the center of the necklace, hook an opened ³/₈" (1cm) jump ring onto a row of knitted stitches, add a drop, then close the ring. Staying on the same row of knitted stitches, skip 3 stitches, then fasten a linked drop onto the necklace in the same fashion. Continue to alternate drops with linked drops every 3 stitches, working outward from the center of the necklace.

Knitted Flower Pin

This pin uses twelve individual pieces of dowel-knitted rope, but they are made as one long rope and then cut apart. Working in this way, rather than making each piece individually, is a real time-saver. Once created, the rope sections are strung onto a continuous wire that is then formed into a floral shape. This is a piece that I recommend for an experienced jewelry maker.

Finished Size: approx. 2¹/₂" (6.4cm) wide

materials list

27 yds. (24.7m) of 28 gauge round wire	20" (50.8cm) of 26 gauge round wire in a base metal of your choice	¹/₄" (6mm) dowel rod
44" (111.8cm) of 18 gauge round wire	8 textured metal 6mm beads	Masking tape
48" (121.9cm) of 26 gauge round wire	10mm × 15mm oval glass faceted bead	

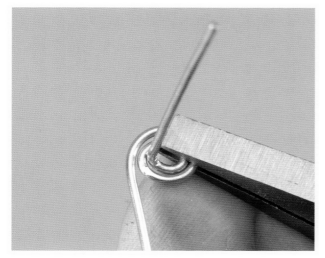

1 Cut a 40" (101.6cm) length of 18 gauge wire. Make a 90 degree bend in the wire 1" (2.5cm) from the end of the wire. This extended length of wire will later act as a bead post. To form a flat coil around the base of the bead post, grasp the wire at the bend with a pair of flat nose pliers. Start turning the wire around the base, then change to round nose pliers to complete the first round of the coil. Continue to make a closed flat coil for a total of 4 rounds. Then, make 2 additional rounds of open coil. Hammer the coil only, not the post or the extra wire (see Hammering on page 18).

2 At the end of the coil, using flat nose pliers, bend the wire at a 90 degree angle away from the coil. Next, make a sharp but slight bend 2¹/₄" (5.7cm) away from the first. Continue to make slight bends along the wire, each 2¹/₄" (5.7cm) away from the previous bend, until there are 12 sections that are 2¹/₄" (5.7cm) long.

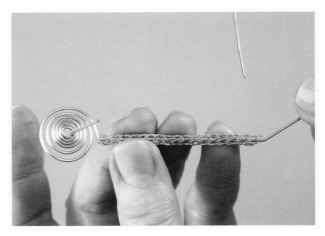

3 Use 20" (50.8cm) of 26 gauge base metal wire to make a 6-petal harness. Tape it to the end of a 1/4" (6mm) dowel rod. Using 28 gauge wire, make a 24" (61cm) long single dowel-knitted rope (see Single Dowel-Knitted Rope on page 124). Pull the dowel-knitted piece through a drawplate until it is approximately 5/16" (8mm) in diameter and at least 30" (76.2cm) long (see Using a Drawplate on page 126).

Keeping the harness intact, cut this rope into 12 pieces, each 2 1/2" (6.4cm) long. Working around the rope for each cut, use side cutters to snip each wire of the weave. Clean up the ends of each length by pulling away any wire bits, then bend the wire ends to the insides of the tubes.

4 String one of the tubes onto the wire extending from the coil and place it within the first 2 1/4" (5.7cm) section (next to the coil).

5 Using your fingers or a dowel rod, shape the petal to round it. Use chain nose pliers to sharply bend the first slight bend to make a V shape in the 18 gauge wire that meets with the coil.

Continue in this manner until there are 12 petals. The petals will overlap, but the sharp bends in the wire should all meet with the coil. Trim off the excess 18 gauge wire and fasten it with a tight loop onto the bottom of the first petal (see Tight Loops on page 21).

6 Fasten a 24" (61cm) length of 26 gauge wire onto the outermost round of the coil with several wraps. Work around the coil with this wire, wrapping the bends of the petals to the outermost coil, using 3 wraps in each sharp bend. As you work, space the petals so they all fit—the bends will fit closely together. End off the 26 gauge wire.

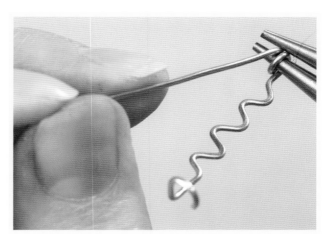

7 Tape the harness from Step 3 back onto the end of the ¼" (6mm) dowel rod. Using 28 gauge wire, make a ½" (1.3cm) long double dowel-knitted rope (see Double Dowel-Knitted Rope on page 125). Remove the rope from the dowel. Fold the wire ends to the inside of the rope. Slide the rope, which will serve as a bezel for the oval bead, onto the oval bead. Compact the end of the bezel to fit the bead. Place the bead onto the post in the center of the flower and trim the wire extending from the bead to ¼" (6mm). Hammer the wire end, taking care not to hit the bead, then bend it to the side and curl it using round nose pliers.

8 Use 4" (10.2cm) of 18 gauge wire to make a 1" (2.5cm) long pin back (see Pin Back on page 29).

9 Fasten a 24" (61cm) length of 26 gauge wire onto the coil at the back of the piece. Position the pin back toward the top of the coil (not across the center—this would cause sagging while wearing). Use the 26 gauge wire to sew both the pin back to the back of the piece and the beads to the front of the piece around the oval bead. Working over the fifth round of the coil, bring the wire through to the front of the piece, string on a bead, bring the wire to the back, then wrap it several times around the coil. Continue until all beads and the pin back are in place. Fasten off the 26 gauge wire. Shape and arrange the petals, curving and overlapping them as you desire.

Lariat Necklace

The challenge of this piece is in dowel knitting with the fine, 32 gauge wire, which makes a more fluid, fabric-like rope than heavier gauges. Use a tapestry needle to work the wire through the stitches to make this project go more smoothly. Choose bead colors to coordinate with or contrast with the colors in the rope. The wire worked parts of this project are simple, but the rope is for experienced dowel knitters.

Finished Size: approx. 27" (68.6cm) long

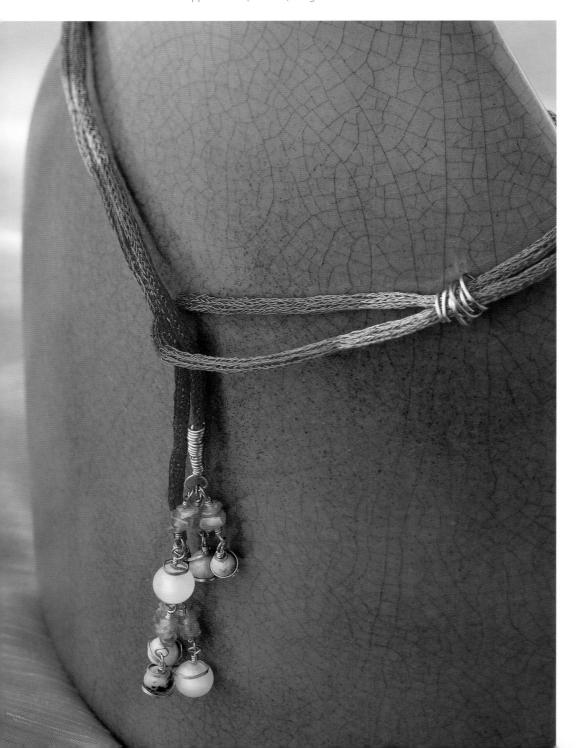

materials list

4 spools, 200 yds. (182.9m) each, of 32 gauge wire, 1 each in natural, orange, red and fuchsia, or in colors of your choice

22" (55.9cm) of 20 gauge round wire

31¹/₂" (80cm) of 22 gauge round wire

20" (50.8cm) of 28 gauge round wire in a base metal of your choice

18 carnelian chip beads

6 round beads of assorted colors and sizes

Size 20 tapestry sewing needle

³/₁₆" (5mm) dowel

Masking tape

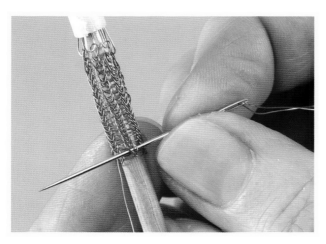

1 Use a 20" (50.8cm) length of 28 gauge base metal wire to make a 6-petal harness. Tape it to the end of a ³/₁₆" (5mm) dowel rod. Cut 36" (91.4cm) of fuschia 32 gauge wire. Use it to begin creating a double dowel-knitted rope (see Double Dowel-Knitted Rope on page 125). Because 32 gauge is very fine, use a sewing needle to bring the wire through the stitches. The fine wire will also tend to kink—remove the kinks before they reach the stitches by running your fingers over the wire to straighten it.

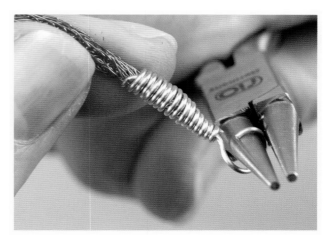

2 When you reach the end of the fuschia wire, continue dowel knitting with a 36" (91.4cm) length of red wire. Make color changes following this pattern: fuschia, red, orange, natural, orange, red. Continue in this sequence until there are 51 color sections, or the piece is about 26" (66cm) long. Pull the dowel-knitted piece through a drawplate until it is approximately 48" (121.9cm) long (see Using a Drawplate on page 126).

Use 8" (20.3cm) of 20 gauge wire to make an end cap and plain loop at one end of the rope (see End Caps and Loops on pages 126–127). Repeat at the other end.

3 Cut 6" (15.2cm) of 20 gauge wire, then hammer the length of it (see Hammering on page 18). Fold the dowel-knitted rope nearly in half with one end approximately 2" (5.1cm) longer than the other. Wrap the hammered wire around the doubled rope 2½" (6.4cm) from the fold. Use pliers to tighten the hammered fastener just enough so it stays in place.

4 Make 6 wrapped bead links using 2¼" (5.7cm) of 22 gauge wire and 3 carnelian chip beads for each (see Bead Links on page 21). Make 6 wrapped bead drops using 3" (7.6cm) of 22 gauge wire and a single round bead for each (see Bead Drops on page 22). Form a wrapped loop in one end, and as you form the wrapped loop attach it to a bead link. String on a round bead, hammer the wire end, then curl it up and over the bead and fasten with a tight loop above the bead. Fasten 3 linked drops onto each end of the rope.

Seed Bead & Crystal Earrings

In this unique pair of earrings, seed beads are added into the dowel-knitting and settle between rows of stitches, adding texture and glitter to the knitted rope. I recommend this project for experienced wire workers and dowel knitters.

Finished Size: approx. 1½" (3.8cm) long × ⅞" (2.2cm) wide

materials list

13 yds. (11.9m) of 28 gauge round wire

24" (61cm) of 22 gauge round wire

5" (12.7cm) of 26 gauge round wire in a base metal of your choice

144 size 11/0 seed beads

2 crystal 8mm beads

Ear wires (see page 25 to make your own)

³/₁₆" (5mm) dowel

Masking tape

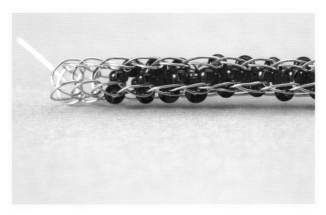

1 Use a 15" (38.1cm) length of 26 gauge base metal wire to make a 4-petal harness. Tape it to the end of a ³/₁₆" (5mm) dowel rod. Use 54" (137.2cm) of 28 gauge wire to work 4 rounds of dowel knitting (see Single Dowel-Knitted Rope on page 124). The first round is a waste round and will be cut away. After these rounds are complete, work 18 rounds with beads; to dowel knit with beads, add a seed bead onto the wire before working each stitch. Finish with 3 more unbeaded rounds. Remove the knitting from the dowel and pull it through a drawplate until it is approximately ¹/₄" (6mm) in diameter (see Using a Drawplate on page 126). Using side cutters, cut away the waste round. Remove any wire bits and finish the wire ends to the inside of the tube.

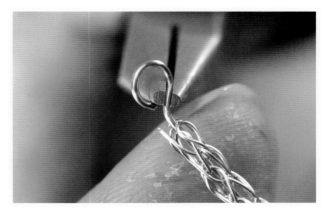

2 Cut a 6" (15.2cm) length of 22 gauge wire. Thread the wire through the tube until ³/₈" (1cm) extends from the end of the tube. Pinch the 3 plain rows of the rope at the top so they lie close to the wire, then form a loop in the ³/₈" (1cm) wire end. Use 6" (15.2cm) of 22 gauge wire to make an end cap without a loop at the same end (see End Caps and Loops on pages 126–127). Cover the tube end completely with the end cap, ending at the base of the loop.

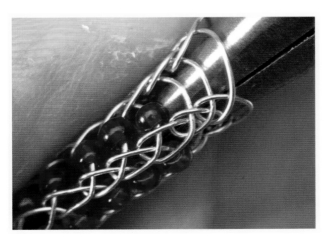

3 Insert a closed pair of chain nose pliers into the open end of the tube and flare it wider, then string the 8mm bead onto the wire.

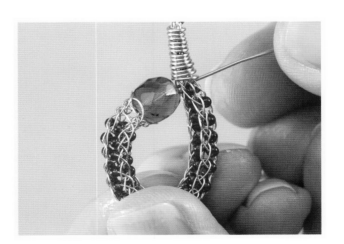

4 Curl the beaded tube and pierce the end of the wire through the tube above the beaded section, then pull the wire snug. Hammer the wire end and wrap it around the end cap, leaving slight gaps between wraps (see Hammering on page 18). Fasten the wire with a tight loop beneath the simple loop (see Tight Loops on page 21). Attach an ear wire to the top loop. Repeat for a second earring.

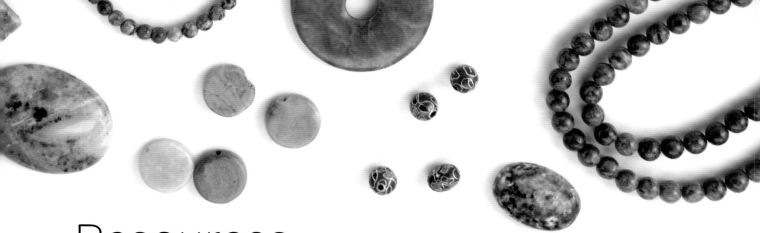

Resources

Most of the items used in this book are easy to find at your local craft stores or bead and jewelry stores, at bead and jewelry shows, and online. When shopping for jewelry-making supplies, I recommend starting with local suppliers as well as bead and jewelry shows. These are the best places to hand-select your materials. Semiprecious beads, cabochons and donuts are all special, and each one is different. Picking them out in person allows you to get exactly the look you want. However, if you don't have a local jewelry supplier, or you can't find what you want locally, bead and wire suppliers are easy to find online, and you can be happily surprised upon opening your box of supplies. If you find yourself trying out wire design ideas and going through lots of base metal wire (as I do!), I suggest buying wire in one-pound spools. You will most likely have to order a larger amount online or through a catalog because most local bead shops only have smaller wire put-ups. Whether you order by mail or not, it can also be useful to have some catalogs on hand to browse through and learn what new and exciting supplies are available—they can be a great source of information! And, of course, websites of suppliers are often packed with helpful information. As you try new techniques and supplies, you're sure to accumulate your own group of trusted resources.

Manufacturers I recommend:

Beadalon
www.beadalon.com
Beading wire, crimp beads, tools, findings

Rio Grande
www.riogrande.com
Base metal and precious wire, semi-precious beads, tools, findings

Paramount Wire Co., Inc.
www.parawire.com
Coated wire in many gauges (including 32 and 34), tools.

Bibliography

Coming up with designs for unique jewelry pieces requires pursuing jewelry as an art form rather than a means of merely acquiring a bauble to wear. For me, a bit of research is where it all begins. Having a collection of design books on hand is one way to surround yourself with inspiration. Other ways are to browse through galleries and shops featuring unique and artful pieces as well as museums and other collections of artifacts. You never know when someone else's creation, from now or from long ago, will spark a totally new idea for you. Here are some of my sources of inspiration:

Dubin, Lois Sherr. *North American Indian Jewelry and Adornment: From Prehistory to the Present, Concise Edition*. New York, NY: Harry N. Abrams, Inc., 2003.

Fisch, Arline M. *Textile Techniques in Metal: For Jewelers, Textile Artists & Sculptors*. Asheville, NC: Lark Books, 1996.

Le Van, Marthe. *The Penland Book of Jewelry: Master Classes in Jewelry Techniques*. Asheville, NC: Lark Books, 2005.

McCreight, Tim. *Jewelry: Fundamentals of Metalsmithing*. Boston, MA: Hand Books Press, 1997.

Romero, Christie. *Warman's Jewelry Identification and Price Guide: A Fully Illustrated Identification and Price Guide to 18th, 19th & 20th Century Fine and Costume Jewelry*. Iola, WI: Krause Publications, 2002.

Untracht, Oppi. *Jewelry: Concepts and Technology*. New York, NY: Doubleday, 1982.

Rower, Alexander S.C., ed. *Calder Jewelry*. New York, NY: Calder Foundation, 2007.

White, Merle, ed. *Lapidary Journal Jewelry Artist* (magazine). Loveland, CO: Interweave Press.

Index

Dedication

I dedicate this book to the earliest masters of wire, those who first figured out how to turn ore into metal and metal into wire, and then to form the stringy stuff into wearable art. It must have taken incredible imagination to create the timeless ancient pieces as can be seen at the Louvre and in other collections.

Acknowledgments

Many, many thanks to the wonderful crew at F+W Media, Inc. for hosting me for a week of delightful lunches and all-day photo shoots. Getting out of the studio has never been so fun! Thanks to editor Jenni Claydon whose professionalism is unparalleled in both her excellent way with words and in keeping things on track (and for all of our wild and woolly conversations!), Christine Polomsky who is a master at getting a photograph right on the first shot (amazing!), Geoff Raker who did the exceptional cover photo and whose font choices I love, Ric Deliantoni for the photographs of the finished jewelry, and Nora Martini and Jennifer Wilson for styling the photos.

What is life without supplies?! I so very much appreciate those who have enhanced my creative spirit with fabulous contributions. Many thanks to Bill Coates of Paramount Wire Co., Inc.; Yvette Rodriguez of Beadalon; Sharon Christenson of Rio Grande; and Shipwreck Beads for tools, beads and supplies that appear throughout this book.

About the Author

J. Marsha Michler has authored twelve books and several magazine articles about her extensive and varied crafting expertise. In addition to actively pursuing quilting, crazy quilting, jewelry making, fiber spinning, knitting, pottery, photography and website design, she also teaches, lectures, signs books and shows her artwork in the New England area. In her spare time she gardens, builds stone walls, travels, and enjoys sushi with her husband. She resides in southern Maine. Her website is www.jmarshamichler.com.

Metric Conversion Chart

To convert	to	multiply by
Inches	Centimeters	2.54
Centimeters	Inches	0.4
Feet	Centimeters	30.5
Centimeters	Feet	0.03
Yards	Meters	0.9
Meters	Yards	1.1

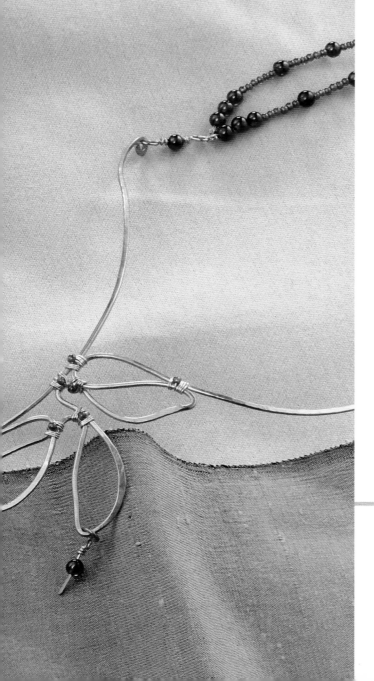

15 14 13 12 11   5 4 3 2 1

DISTRIBUTED IN CANADA BY FRASER DIRECT
100 Armstrong Avenue
Georgetown, ON, Canada L7G 5S4
Tel: (905) 877-4411

DISTRIBUTED IN THE U.K. AND EUROPE BY
F&W MEDIA INTERNATIONAL
Brunel House, Newton Abbot, Devon, TQ12 4PU,
England
Tel: (+44) 1626 323200, Fax: (+44) 1626 323319
Email: enquiries@fwmedia.com

DISTRIBUTED IN AUSTRALIA BY CAPRICORN
LINK
P.O. Box 704, S. Windsor NSW, 2756 Australia
Tel: (02) 4577-3555

SRN: Z9354
ISBN-13: 978-1-4402-1406-6

www.fwmedia.com

Edited by Jennifer Claydon
Designed by Geoff Raker
Production coordinated by Greg Nock
Photography by Christine Polomsky & Ric Deliantoni
Styling by Jennifer Wilson & Nora Martini

Find free bonus projects online!

Visit CreateMixedMedia.com/art-of-wire-free-patterns to get free instructions for these gorgeous bonus projects.

Check out these essential wire-working titles from North Light Books!

Create 30 stepped-out projects that explore the possibilities for using wire as a dimensional design feature as well as a structural one through combinations of both hard and soft wire.

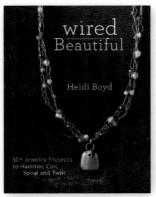

Learn the ins and outs of working with wire and enjoy Heidi Boyd's fresh design approach and great techniques.

NORTH LIGHT BOOKS

 fwcraft

 @fwcraft

These and other fine jewelry-making titles are available in craft and book stores, or visit **ShopMixedMedia.com**

:11

▶ Get Ready

CUTTING • STAMPING • BALLING WIRE • FORMING
DRILLING • SAWING • RIVETING

▶▶ Get Set

Plastic folder, any color

Sterling silver round wire,
18 gauge, 1 inch
(2.5 cm)

Sterling silver disk,
22 gauge, ¼ inch
(6 mm)

Sterling silver tube,
1 mm ID (interior
diameter), 2.05 mm
OD (outside diameter),
7.12 mm long

Solvent inkpad

Rubber stamp

Bench tool kit, page 9

Soldering kit, page 9

FINISHED SIZE
7 x 7 x 3.8 cm

▶▶▶ Go

1. Use scissors to cut the folder into six plastic strips, each ½ x 8¼ inches (1.3 x 21 cm) long.

2. Line up the strips on a flat surface in parallel rows, and tape them down. Using the inkpad and a rubber stamp, create a pattern on the strips. Once the ink dries, seal it with matte spray fixative.

3. Use a permanent marker to mark the center of one end of each strip, 5 mm from the edge. Mark a spot on the opposite end of each strip that is slightly off center, 5 mm from the edge. Round the ends with scissors, or snip each corner at an angle.

4. Use a torch to ball one end of the 1-inch (2.5 cm) 18-gauge wire.

5. Thread the wire through a corresponding hole in a drawplate. Use a chasing hammer to flatten the ball, making a headpin.

6. Drill a 1-mm hole in the ¼-inch (6 mm) silver disk. Drill a 1-mm hole at each marked spot on the strips.

7. Gather the strips together. Thread the headpin through one hole at a time, making sure to overlap the strips in a pleasing manner and to secure each strip in a complete circle. Thread the drilled ¼-inch (6 mm) disk onto the headpin, and trim the remaining wire to a good length for riveting. Rivet the wire.

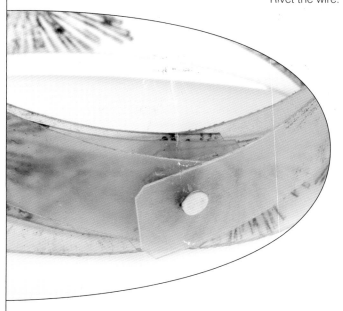